GOD'S HAND

IN THE LIFE OF A PASTOR

GOD'S HAND

IN THE LIFE OF A PASTOR

Jimmy Yamada, Jr.

WHITE
MOUNTAIN
CASTLE
PUBLISHING, LLC

www.whitemountaincastle.com
Kapolei, Hawai'i

GOD'S HAND

IN THE **LIFE** OF A **PASTOR**

Copyright © 2015 Jimmy Yamada, Jr.
Published by White Mountain Castle Publishing, LLC

WHITE
MOUNTAIN
CASTLE
PUBLISHING, LLC

White Mountain Castle Publishing, LLC
P.O. Box 700833
Kapolei, Hawaii 96709

Email: whitemountaincastle@yahoo.com
Website: whitemountaincastle.com

Edited by Dawn O'Brien
Cover Design & Text Formatting by Sherrie Dodo
Cover Photos by ©iStockphoto.com
Back Cover Photo by Marc Schecther

ISBN 978-0-9815219-4-7

Printed in Korea

DEDICATION

To Pastor Klayton Ko whom I sat under for most of my
developing Christian life. He is always there at all of my life's
turning points. He also gave me freedom to grow and go after
extracurricular (Christian) activities. Pastor Klayton has
trailblazed foundational Christian principles, and introduced
me to them by bringing in David Barton as a speaker and
writer. I didn't think it affected me then; I'm slow.

Also to Pastor Allen Cardines who is trailblazing in the
political arena and believing for a better America. He keeps
the body of Christ connected to our government because he's
sincerely concerned with people and how they're impacted.
Not one to "just leave it in God's Hands," Allen re-awakens
us all to the foundational structures of this book — both the
Constitution and the Bible upon which it was founded.

And to Pastors John Roger and Tom Bauer whom God used
to encourage me on my journey to becoming a pastor. God
also used Pastor Tom to give me a heart for the poor. Agape!

TABLE OF CONTENTS

PREFACE

LIFE AS A PASTOR SEES IT

Growing up, I dreamt big dreams and imagined great accomplishments. My mom called me, "Shooting Star," bright for a second, then fizzle! Becoming a pastor was never one of my ultimate goals. I never dreamed of my name in lights: **Pastor Jimmy Yamada!** Yet here I am, a senior citizen and a senior pastor. And our church? Far from fame and fortune; rather, it is rich in faith and in people living in poverty.

This is not a book about my life (although it will, naturally, include that). Instead, I invite you to look at our nation: where we *were*, where we *are*, and where we are *headed*. The goal? Simple: To face urgent issues we all struggle with today. There is a deep-and-vital connection between the issues impacting America, God's Hand upon our nation, the poor of our country, and every single one of us.

My insight is from "the view below": looking to God above to give wisdom through His Word as well as through the journey on which He has lead me. I'm pastor of **Cedar Assembly of God** yet I've also learned many life lessons from business as former president and current CEO of **A-1 A-Lectrician, Inc.** God has worked for my good all of my life, especially changing my focus over the past seven years. He has given me a good but poor congregation, not just so that I can bring to them a living Gospel, but that He could make the Gospel come alive for me. Why? So that I may become more like Jesus. I invite you to join me in my journey, past, present and future knowing that we will grow in Christ together.

PURPOSE OF THE BOOK

Nick Vujicic, the evangelist without limbs, once told of a young boy innocently noticing his missing arms and legs. The boy asked, "What happened?" Nick answered: "Smoking!"

This book asks a similar question, ***"What happened to America?"*** Once the greatest, richest, most powerful nation on earth, the whole world looked up to America! "What happened?" My first thought: "Smoking!"

Seriously, if you're wondering the same, keep reading. ***Is God involved in some way?*** Is He trying to teach us something? Or does He want something from us?

Business experience has taught me to use the Peter Drucker model: **Ask questions.** This book seeks answers by asking questions. My goal is to ask the ***right*** questions. That way we can all individually come to our own conclusions and, hopefully, the right answers. Part of my focus will be the poor because that's where God has me, but the applications are universal: we all have poor in our lives.

Questions include:
* What is causing America's problems?
* Who is responsible?
* Are there solutions?
* Is God involved in these problems?
    * Could these "problems" be opportunities for God to work

things out for our good? If so, what might that good look like?
* Is America in trouble because of the poor? Or because of the rich?
* Is America in trouble because Christians have neglected our duty? If so, what duty did God give Christians to keep America on track?
* Is America in trouble because it has abandoned God?
* Is God trying to awaken American Christians to the realities of living life in the Last Days?

QUESTIONS RELATING TO THE POOR

God called me to minister to the poorest of the poor, so I'll include what I have learned about the poor. Admittedly, I have a bias and will conclude with how I (we?) might live among our poor. We all have poor in our lives. Homelessness is a huge issue in Hawaii, but I will expand the concept of the poor beyond the homeless.

Questions:
* Can we solve the problem of the homeless and the poor?
* Is this a problem to be solved by embracing a new way of living?
* What if there are no solutions to homelessness and it just gets worse?
* What if those living in shelters/rooming houses continue to pass in and out of homelessness?
* What if the costs of government housing increases fivefold or tenfold in the next 10-20 years? What impact will that have on America as our nation's finances are already near breaking point?
* What impact will that have on the rest of us? Is there a way out?

* Why are so many in the middle class having such a difficult time surviving?
* Why does the middle class seem to be moving backward in standard of living?
* Why are so many college graduates not able to find jobs commensurate to their education?
* Is it possible for the bottom to fall out from a large portion of the middle class, so that they become poor &/or homeless?
* What is the social impact on America if the middle class falls below the poverty level?
* Can college graduates end up poor? Including those who are middle-aged and senior citizens?
* What if we will all die one day? (Got you!)
* Are many terrified or at least terribly inconvenienced at the prospect of death?
* What kind of fears do normal people have in approaching death?
* How might we look at death from God's view?
* Is there a difference between knowing, living and walking through difficult times?
* Are there answers or is God in trouble? Has He bitten off more than He can chew? Is He really in control?
* Are we all really poor trying to be rich?

STYLE

The subject matter is tough, controversial, and not necessarily truth as presented. Allow me to explain: one of the top financial gurus in the world, John Mauldin, once said, "Correlation is not causation." Just because facts seem to line up and it appears that Event A causes Event B to happen 10 times in a row, it may not necessarily be so. We may be able to line up logic, track it on charts, and clearly show correlation that summarily jumps to a conclusion. I may be guilty of violating John Mauldin's statement but it's my book. Sorry, no refunds!

I embrace the relational method, or what I call, "tuning fork Christianity."

From Wikipedia:

"A tuning fork is an <u>acoustic resonator</u> in the form of a two-pronged <u>fork</u> with the prongs (<u>tines</u>) formed from a U-shaped bar of <u>elastic</u> metal (usually <u>steel</u>). It <u>resonates</u> at a specific constant <u>pitch</u> when set vibrating by striking it against a surface or with an object, and emits a pure musical tone after waiting a moment to allow some high <u>overtones</u> to die out. The pitch that a particular tuning fork generates depends on the length and mass of the two prongs. It is frequently used as a standard of pitch to tune musical instruments."

When two identical tuning forks are placed next to each other, striking one and placing it next to the other will cause the other tuning fork to resonate at the same frequency. So if what I present resonates with you, great. Let's resonate together: "*Hmmmmmmmm.*"

If you add a weight to the stationary tuning fork, and strike the other, the stationary one will now have a different frequency due to the weight and will not resonate. If you have similar thoughts but are carrying different weights (your heart or passion), you will not resonate and embrace what I am presenting. That's okay; we're still family. Even Diana, my wife, doesn't resonate with me on all my "cockamamie" ideas.

MY HEART

Proverbs 12:23, "*A prudent man keeps his knowledge to himself....*"
Or, "If you think you know, you dunno," (1 Corinthians 8:1, Jimmy's version).
Diana might say: "You think you know everything."

I would counter: "She has me wrong. I have opinions on everything, so remember, it's just my opinion!"

The focus is the impact on the poor. God chose me for the poor. He is humbling me. While I was "head honcho" at my company, everyone listened to me. Many loved me but they also loved their paychecks. Now, I'm truly blessed if some of my congregation pay attention when I'm preaching.

For example, I preach on **agape** (unconditional love) often, but right after service, security has rushed to handle serious disturbances. Another example: Typically I ask: "What did I teach on last week?" No one remembers, except my pastoral team (I love them). Humbling, but I've learned to trust God more. That's got to be good.

God also wants me to understand the signs of the times, so my opinions will focus mainly around what is causing the poor to be poor. I will try to analyze this from God's perspective to see if God might be involved. But I've also learned just because I can pull out a relevant Scripture, my conclusion may not be God's truth. That said, my hope is that we can all understand better what God is doing.

POOR DEFINED

Jesus said: *"The poor you will always have with you, but you will not always have me,"* (Matthew 26:11).

What did He mean by "the poor?" In all of the Bible's lessons, God does not give us conditions and guidelines for overlooking the poor. However, He does talk about drunkenness and laziness as sin. Does that mean if people are poor and lazy, or alcoholics or drug addicts, we don't have to feed them or give them drink?

One of the difficulties we all face is trying to practically live out God's teachings. It's often confusing to understand His heart when all the Scriptures seem "meshed" together. What am I saying? Think of it this way: Take all the Scriptures on a subject, and try to apply them to how to live, and I often draw a blank.

Then I think, "Oh, goody, I'll just ignore the ones I don't like, the ones that make it difficult to live for today. Tomorrow is another day!"

This book is an attempt to lay out how I might live among the poor with everything "meshed" together. I may fall short as I try to incorporate all the different conditions and situations in the world; after all, who can incorporate what is happening globally, economically, financially, socially, and come up with a life plan and mission for a particular group of people, in this case the poor. Since I've set myself up with an impossible task, I cannot fail, because I already said it's impossible.

However, since nothing is impossible with God, I'll bring God into the picture and see if He can help us find our way.

FOUR TYPES OF POVERTY

Ed Silvoso defines four types of poverty: ("Transformation", Regal Books, Ventura, CA, p. 117)

"1. **Spiritual poverty** afflicts those who do not know that God is their father.

2. **Relational poverty** encompasses those whose focus is on themselves at the expense of the community they are a part of.

3. **Motivational poverty** is a state of hopelessness that engulfs those who have no adequate way or means (or the confidence) to tackle tomorrow's challenges.

4. **Material poverty** impacts those who lack the basic necessities to sustain themselves."

FIVE GROUPS OF POOR (Yikes, I'm one of them!)

Let's break the "poor" into 5 distinct groups to help systematically deal with the issue. This will give us a tangible, realistic way of analyzing each group and discussing the way world situations impact them.

XIV

Each group has special conditions, different culture, unique circumstances and *almost* unsolvable challenges. Those challenges may flow into other groups, but I'll attempt to deal with primary issues impacting each one.

We are all "poor" in some way because we are not perfect like Jesus. We all have emotional baggage, deep hurts, needs or traumatic experiences that creates in us a "normally poor" condition. God allows us to go through pain and suffering to draw us to Him. Emptiness, loneliness, fear and guilt are what God allows so that we continually seek Him. Most of us eventually adapt, with or without Jesus, although those who have Jesus adapt better. I will not be dealing with the "normally poor," as we are all throughout society and not distinguishable as a group.

The five groups:

1. THE HOMELESS POOR
The first group is the most obvious: the homeless. This includes people without homes, the soon-to-be homeless, those living in shelters, and those living in rented rooms. They become homeless on a moment's notice, at a landlord's discretion. Hawaii and the entire nation are looking for solutions to the homeless problem.

2. THOSE IN POVERTY (BUT NOT HOMELESS)
The second group of poor include those who are living in a rental, public housing, Section 8 housing, who are below the poverty level. They have government assistance such as food stamps (SNAP), welfare, disability (SSD), and Medicaid coverage.

3. MIDDLE CLASS POOR (& HEADED TO POVERTY)
The third group is the middle class who have been losing purchasing power for the past 10-15 years, have income, some assets, little savings, and very little retirement. (Obviously, not all middle class fall

into this group). They have little hope of breaking out of their condition and will end up struggling during "golden" retirement years. Most likely, they'll end up working into their 70s. Some may be a paycheck or two from being homeless. If one or both income providers lose their job, they'll end up homeless. Too often one is struck with a medical condition, and the other loses their income.

4. COLLEGE GRADUATES ("EDUCATED POOR")

The fourth group are the educated poor, those who have gone to college yet do not have the jobs they were expecting. They're also the professional (including white collar workers) in their 50s who lost jobs in the recession.

In his groundbreaking book, the "Failure of Laissez Faire Capitalism," Paul Craig Roberts tells us that the college graduate in this group may increase by 6-8 million (or more) over the next 7-10 years. The book and its warning were released in early 2013.

The elderly professionals in this group went to college 30 years ago. Their future bosses are in their 30s, thinking "this guy looks old." These college graduates have a severe case of "soul hurt." And unless things change dramatically for this group, America is in for some big time hurt. The ramifications are many and severe.

5. THE DYING POOR

This fifth group includes many since we all will die. This includes anyone (Christian and nonbeliever) fearful of dying as well as the terminally ill, who worry about living through the "dying experience." It also includes those who will have a prolonged period of difficulty in their last years: pain and suffering, dementia, Alzheimer's, cancer, dialysis, etcetera. Even Christians may have anxiety or fear about this season of life.

Are you prepared? Is Jesus enough for you as you enter your twilight years? Or will it truly be a death spiral? This season can be your golden years (because you will see Jesus soon) or the worst period of your life. Can you relate to Paul when he wrote: *"For to me, to live is Christ and to die is gain"* (Philippians 1:21)? If you do, then you will handle death well; you do not fall into this group.

CAN THE POOR PROBLEM BE SOLVED? IS THERE HOPE?

Jesus said: *"The poor you will always have with you, but you will not always have me,"* (Matthew 26:11).

God has a good plan for us. He is moving and we see the result of His Hand throughout our daily lives. God never does anything without a purpose. We may not always see His Hand because we don't understand how He works and do not see through His eyes. Too often I'm oblivious to the things of God when blinded by the sweetness of the world.

I've come to realize that He awakened me to the poor. There are many other ways God can work for good in people's lives. This is just the model He decided to use for my good. He connected me to the poor to humble me; perhaps He can help you once you realize His workings in your life.

WHAT DOES GOD DESIRE? HOW SHOULD WE LIVE?

God reveals His desires in His Word, therefore, for answers we must look to His Word. God desires that we help the poor: those hungry, thirsty, strangers with no place to stay (homeless), those in need of clothes, the sick, and those in prison; it is as if we're caring for Jesus Himself (Mt. 25:34-40).

God describes true fasting: Isaiah 58:3-8   (MY COMMENTS, %)
"'Why have we fasted,' they say,
'and you have not seen it?

Why have we humbled ourselves,
and you have not noticed?'

"Yet on the day of your fasting, you do as you please
and exploit all your workers.
4 Your fasting ends in quarreling and strife,   (THAT'S ME)
and in striking each other with wicked fists.
You cannot fast as you do today
and expect your voice to be heard on high.
5 Is this the kind of fast I have chosen,
only a day for a man to humble himself?   (GUILTY)
Is it only for bowing one's head like a reed
and for lying on sackcloth and ashes?   (GUILTY)
Is that what you call a fast,
a day acceptable to the Lord?

6 "Is not this the kind of fasting I have chosen:
to loose the chains of injustice   (NOT THERE)
and untie the cords of the yoke,   (NOT THERE)
to set the oppressed free
and break every yoke?
7 Is it not to share your food with the hungry   (NOT THERE)
and to provide the poor wanderer with shelter —   (NOT THERE)
when you see the naked, to clothe him,   (NOT THERE)
and not to turn away from your own flesh and blood?
8 Then your light will break forth like the dawn,   (HOPE I GET THERE)
and your healing will quickly appear;
then your righteousness will go before you...."

Could it be that our Jesus is different from the Jesus of the Bible? A song by Todd Agnew entitled, "My Jesus," asks that very question:

MY JESUS   (MY COMMENTS)
Which Jesus do you follow?

Which Jesus do you serve?
If Ephesians says to imitate Christ
Then why do you look so much like the world?   (GUILTY)

Cause my Jesus bled and died
He spent His time with thieves and liars   (NOT THERE YET)
He loved the poor and accosted the arrogant
So which one do you want to be?   (I WANNA BE)

Blessed are the poor in spirit
Or do we pray to be blessed with the wealth of this land (GUILTY)
Blessed are they that hunger and thirst for righteousness
Or do we ache for another taste of this world of shifting sand   (☹)

Cause my Jesus bled and died for my sins   (☹)
He spent His time with thieves and sluts and liars
He loved the poor and accosted the rich
So which one do you want to be?   (☹)

Who is this that you follow
This picture of the American dream

If Jesus was here would you walk right by on the other side   (☹)
or fall down and worship at His holy feet (WOULD I RECOGNIZE HIM?)

Pretty blue eyes and curly brown hair and a clear complexion
Is how you see Him as He dies for your sins
But the Word says He was battered and scarred
Or did you miss that part   (☹)
Sometimes I doubt we'd recognize Him   (GUILTY)

Cause my Jesus bled and died
He spent His time with thieves and the least of these
He loved the poor and accosted the comfortable
So which one do you want to be?

Cause my Jesus would never be accepted in my church   (☹)
The blood and dirt on His feet might stain the carpet
But He reaches for the hurting and despised the proud
I think He'd prefer Beale St. to the stained glass crowd
And I know that He can hear me if I cry out loud

I want to be like my Jesus!   (YES)
I want to be like my Jesus!

IS IT POSSIBLE TO LIVE LIKE JESUS?

Jesus said, *"Be perfect, therefore, as your heavenly Father is perfect,"* (Matthew 5:48). Since Jesus knows we will never be perfect (this side of eternity), I believe He is trying to teach us an eternal lesson.

Peter detailed how we might shoot for this perfection: (2 Peter 1:3-9) *"His divine power has given us everything we need for life and godliness through our knowledge of him who called us by his own glory and goodness. Through these he has given us his very great and precious promises, so that through them you may participate in the divine nature and escape the corruption in the world caused by evil desires.*

"For this very reason, make every effort to add to your faith goodness; and to goodness, knowledge; and to knowledge, self-control; and to self-control, perseverance; and to perseverance, godliness; and to godliness, brotherly kindness; and to brotherly kindness, love. For if you possess these qualities in increasing measure, they will keep you from being ineffective and unproductive in your knowledge of our Lord Jesus Christ. But if anyone does not have them, he is nearsighted and blind, and has forgotten that he has been cleansed from his past sins."

The key word is **"effort"**: **we make every effort to shoot for perfection**. In my book "How To Thrive in An Economic Disaster," I present the case that it is the **being** (becoming like Christ) not the *doing* that is crucial. However, we cannot become like Christ with prayer alone — by staying in our prayer closets, by remaining within the confines of our churches, by pouring out Jesus' love only upon our family.

Family is important; churches are important; and we can grow tremendously by taking care of God's business in these areas. Yet as we shoot for perfection, we must *"...Go and make disciples of all nations, baptizing them in the name of the Father and of the Son and of the Holy Spirit, and teaching them to obey everything I have commanded you,"* (Matthew 28:19-20).

It is by going **beyond family and church** that God has an opportunity to *"convict (us)...of guilt in regard to sin and righteousness and judgment..."* (John 16:8). As we minister to people God chooses for us to reach, we struggle and realize we need Jesus, that we must put our faith in Him. And as we grow in faith, we start doing good works which have already been prepared for us by Him.

If we expect to share our faith, we need to grow in knowledge of Jesus, the Bible, and Christian teaching. We must also express our faith by living with those God has selected for us to minister to in such a way that they become disciples of Jesus. Then we'll see that there is no one "good," and our temper, patience, and anger is tested. Unless we develop self-control, we may say, "I'm outta here! I've had enough of this jerk." However, when we gain self-control by repeatedly crying out to Jesus: "Lord, I need you," we gain perseverance. Then we become more like Jesus, gaining a measure of godliness.

Then we wake up the next day, and start over.

As you come to know Jesus, and everything He did becomes increasingly real, you'll also recognize that He truly has given us *"everything we need for life and godliness."*

This, however, **only becomes real for those who go into the world and reach out to people, including families and church**

families, but also beyond. Becoming like Jesus is the goal. And that requires going to God to continue working for the good of others, and allowing Him to work good within our own souls to help us *"become like His Son."*

"And we know that God causes everything to work together for the good of those who love God and are called according to his purpose for them. For God knew his people in advance, and he chose them to become like his Son..." (Romans 8:28-29 NLT).

GOD HAS A PLAN

TO KNOW THE FATHER = ETERNAL LIFE

John 17:1-5
After Jesus said this, he looked toward heaven and prayed:
"Father, the time has come. Glorify your Son, that your Son may glorify you. For you granted him authority over all people that he might give eternal life to all those you have given him. Now this is eternal life: that they may know you, the only true God, and Jesus Christ, whom you have sent. I have brought you glory on earth by completing the work you gave me to do. And now, Father, glorify me in your presence with the glory I had with you before the world began."

Barnes Commentary on John 17:3: "This is life eternal — This is the source of eternal life; or it is in this manner that it is to be obtained. The knowledge of God and of his Son Jesus Christ is itself a source of unspeakable and eternal joy. Compare John 11:25; John 6:63; John 12:50.
"Might know thee" — The word *"know"* here, as in other places, expresses more than a mere speculative acquaintance with the character and perfections of God. It includes all the impressions on the mind and life which a just view of God and of the Saviour is fitted

to produce. It includes, of course, love, reverence, obedience, honor, gratitude, supreme affection. To know God "as he is" is to know and regard him as a lawgiver, a sovereign, a parent, a friend. It is to yield the whole soul to him, and strive to obey his law." (Albert Barnes, edited By Robert Frew, published by Blackie & Son, London, 1884-85)

CONNECT THE DOTS

All of God's missions, ministries and plans have the ultimate purpose of helping us become like Jesus. God's plan for me was not that I would accomplish great things for Him. He doesn't need my help to do great things. It's to get me to love people more, to gain compassion, and to love as Jesus loves (*Agape* Love). The ministry is important but it was secondary to my own slow transformation.

In fact, all the things that God called me to be involved in, all my meetings, lunches and dinners (woe is me!), Youth for Christ, Surfing the Nations, life groups, men's groups, pastors groups, Salvation Army — all of these were with the ultimate goal of seeing like Jesus, having His heart, His Agape. I have a long way to go, but I have a target that aligns with God's target.

As I have ministered these past seven years to the poorest of the poor, I realize that some are transformed and have new lives. Many more have come to salvation but are satisfied living just the way they are. I can see that I had very little control over their destinies. I will say that as I taught, preached, prayed, and ministered, it was only when God showed up and did something that was any there transformation.

One clear example I often recall happened at the Salvation Army. A person came to thank me for my classes. I asked, "If you were in the same class 10 years ago, do you think it would have made a difference, knowing how you were?" The answer: "No!"

Only God makes any impact: *"I planted the seed, Apollos watered it, but **God made it grow**. So neither he who plants nor he who waters is anything, but only God, who makes things grow"* (1 Corinthians 3:6-7).

"...*Being confident of this, that he who began a good work in you will carry it on to completion until the day of Christ Jesus...*" (Philippians 1:6).

"*Therefore, my dear friends, as you have always obeyed — not only in my presence, but now much more in my absence — continue to work out your salvation with fear and trembling, for it is God who works in you to will and to act according to his good purpose*" (Philippians 2:12-13).

"*And he who searches our hearts knows the mind of the Spirit, because the Spirit intercedes for the saints in accordance with God's will.*

And we know that in all things God works for the good of those who love him, who have been called according to his purpose. For those God foreknew he also predestined to be conformed to the likeness of his Son, that he might be the firstborn among many brothers...

Who is he that condemns? Christ Jesus, who died — more than that, who was raised to life — is at the right hand of God and is also interceding for us" (Romans 8:27-35).

This is a **HUGE** passage about the transformational work of God in our lives. The Holy Spirit is interceding for us (Rom. 8:27), Jesus is interceding for us (Rom. 8:34), the Father desires to conform us to His Son, so it is a "slam dunk" that we slowly move towards becoming like Jesus. It's all God's work.

God does this by interacting with us in every aspect of life, causing all things to work together for our good. He orchestrates situations, working out good even in bad situations. He speaks to us in dreams and visions, and encourages us by using signs and wonders. He gives us wisdom and knowledge, and increases our faith. He also helps us to pray in the Spirit, and edifies us so we gain revelation through the Holy Spirit. And ultimately? We love Him more and more, knowing more about Him, and we grow in giving all for Him.

ARE THE POOR SATISFIED WITH LIFE?

Some Christians are satisfied *"escaping through the flames"* (1 Cor. 3:15) and are fine with the blessings they receive from God, and not really concerned with potential rewards later in heaven. I must confess, I am one of these, to a certain extent. You see, a "buffet Christian" is one who believes in our Lord, Jesus Christ, and is saved by grace. But they tend to pick and choose Scriptures that are convenient to live out.

Sure, I've grown in the number of Scriptures I live out, but still fall far short of perfection. I'll call that "my gap." Everyone has a gap. My hope is to someday close my gap before God takes me.

Death is a subject not far from my thoughts as I'm now 67 and my mom is 89. In fact, God took my dad in 1979, my wife Diana's mom in 1994, her dad in 2002; death isn't foreign to me. It has become exponentially real: my mom has dementia and is close to being bedridden. She is relatively wealthy, yet when I see her on her bed or trying to walk, she could be considered poor. She cannot go out, except to the doctor or hospital, and relationships are limited to immediate family, a close friend, and caregivers. One can be rich and yet poor.

Mom has her good days. She was a strong role model when dad passed away, and especially how she has lived without him for the past 35 years. I can thank her for helping me reach my dream and we can laugh a little together. We laugh, and she is rich. Yet it's her bad days — her "poverty" — that have developed my Christianity. I see how God uses the poor.

However, I cannot spend the same time with all the dying poor in my church. This is my "gap."

ENABLING & ITS NEGATIVE IMPACT

Some Christian "poor" are satisfied to the following extent: They feel that the additional effort and risk — of losing what they have from the government — is not worth taking. Some take advantage of Social Security disability to the tune of $700/month, receive food stamps, and have access to Medicaid. It is difficult for them to go back to work and jump off the gravy train. What if they lose their job? It may be almost impossible to regain disability status.

The same applies to the mother of multiple children who currently has welfare, food stamps, and medical coverage. She cannot marry the father of her kids, so she's stuck in "limbo land," unable to break out of her situation.

Additionally, some have very poor work habits and people skills since they've not developed them over their lifetime, possibly over 30-50 years. Theirs is a wasted life; yet God can still use them, even if they may die homeless or in poverty.

When I think about my gap, is God pleased that I will spend more time with my mom as she is in her last stages of life than I will with others in the same boat? I have a constant flow of people in my church that get hospitalized. Some go into the hospital and come out; some don't come out and we get word that God took them. Is God pleased with me if I never had the chance to visit? Am I unrighteous for rationalizing and justifying by comparing the wasted life of the homeless against the precious life of a mom who raised me? I struggle through my gap.

ARE WE ALL POOR?

Is it possible that we are all poor in some way?

Many are looking for solutions to poverty issues. However, is it possible we may be more productive if we start looking upward and inward? Seeking what God has planned, what He desires, and what our focus should be?

A few of the poor are looking for God to deliver them from their condition, rather than deepening their relationship with God. To the homeless, qualifying for Social Security is like getting a fresh breath from God; however, it is not new life. Many have been "enabled by government," who thereby become disabled.

Some of the poor come to church with the same thinking: **What can you do for me?** *You're supposed to help me. What kind of church doesn't help people?*

These people are not looking for Jesus. They think they've already found Him as they've been born again, and again, and again. Many of the poor have been saved multiple times. This is not to say they are not truly saved. Yet it's hard to tell due to their lifestyles: *"faith without works is dead"* (James 2:26).

For many their lot is so hard that all they want is a momentary reprieve: a shower, food, air conditioning, a friend, some love and respect. Then they walk down our lane and I hope to see them another day. Funny, they don't look the same leaving our home as when they came. Life is hard. I do not judge them.

The bottom line? No matter what the church does to reach out, many will stay homeless and die homeless. Many in public housing, especially those that grew up there, may never find good, consistent work. These young ones will likely end up homeless or in poverty in 10, 20, or 30 years. Still, Christians must work tirelessly to help them improve their spiritual, material, emotional and motivational situation. We leave the results to God.

MORE QUESTIONS

1. How might we thrive viewing things from God's view?
"In Him (is) Life" (John 1:4).
Living life through Christ involves recognizing that He is with us, and if we love and trust Him completely each group will thrive in their circumstances. (None is there, but God wants us there.)

2. When things get bad, are we still able to love God? How do we live if we align our hearts with God's heart? Do we think God is a giant genie in the sky, or Creator who works good for us?

Can we live like Habbakuk: *"Though the fig tree does not bud and there are no grapes on the vines, though the olive crop fails and the fields produce no food, though there are no sheep in the pen and no cattle in the stalls, yet I will rejoice in the Lord, I will be joyful in God my Savior. The Sovereign Lord is my strength; he makes my feet like the feet of a deer, he enables me to go on the heights,"* (Habbakuk 3:17-19).

If I lost everything, could I still rejoice in the Lord? I think not. That must mean that I am no different from the poor that the government enables. The only difference is I have and because I have, I rejoice. Maybe if those in poverty had what I have, and our roles were switched, I would hold on to what I had tightly and not let go of my Social Security disability benefits. Maybe I would very easily become "enabled." My gap just became HUGE.

Do we recognize that to be at peace with God through all conditions of life — rich or poor, He desires that we align our hearts and minds with His? That His will must become our will: *"Thy will be done,"* is easier said than done.

As I approach eternity, some of His words and life's lessons become increasingly relevant in my daily walk. Small thoughts have big impact as my perspective changes. It's a lot like a physics experiment: If you look through a lens from 12 inches away, everything looks small. But when you put your eyes right on the lens, suddenly everything is clear, and HUGE!

The closer I get to eternity, the clearer God's words become. Also, my relationship with God the Father, Son, and Holy Spirit deepens. And, family relationships have become more important too.

Join me in my journey.

CHAPTER 1

GOD IS WORKING FOR OUR GOOD

"God causes everything to work together for
the good of those who love God and are called
according to his purpose for them.
For God knew his people in advance, and he chose
them to become like his Son...."
(Romans 8:28-29 NLT)

MY JOURNEY

My first date with Diana Enokawa was at Rainbow Rollerland, a skating rink on Keeaumoku Street. I'd fallen topsy-turvy over Diana at Roosevelt High School. She was the cutest girl in school and I floated on air anytime I got within 50 feet of her. I didn't even have to see her, I would just sense she was around the corner, and I launched for outer space.

I don't remember much about Roosevelt High, but I do remember Diana's house on School Street. Nothing naughty; in fact, the house was barren. It had a TV in the living room and a few loaded bookshelves; and in the kitchen was a park bench and one table with chairs. No sofas, no coffee tables, no pictures or any décor for that matter.

The neat thing is that I didn't think of how sparse her home was; I was so stoked on Diana that her glow blinded me. God's Hand was already moving: He was developing my heart for the poor. It's not about material goods, but about a person's heart. My mom used to tell me, "Marry a girl with a good heart." And Diana has a good heart.

Although her family was poor (not in poverty; they were not on welfare), they had a special relationship with one another. They stood together. Though their home was simple, God used the specialness of their family. I learned that there are things much more important than money. This paralleled my mom's teaching. However, God knows we need practical life lessons beyond parental guidance. There's something about living life together that makes God's lesson come alive in our souls. And living life with the Enokawas awakened my soul.

I remember many nights sitting around the kitchen table listening and watching them tell stories, eat snacks, and laugh all night. What surprised me was how they could tell story after story, on and on, all night long. But the laughter was contagious. No one could sit with them and not laugh. "Remember the time," someone would say, and someone else would jump in and add something — either more of the same story, or something entirely different, and on to a new direction they would head.

The topic never mattered. If you wanted to chime in, you had to jump in quick or you'd find yourself in the wrong story. It was a bit difficult as I was not yet part of their stories, but it didn't matter; laughter doesn't care.

The Enokawas were always moving, and the next place they moved was near Alapai Street. We were in college by then. Again the house was an old one, probably dating back to the 1920s. They had front steps, metal roofing, and a small one-way lane of narrow asphalt. Trees covered the five houses on the lane and their falling leaves kept the dirt from getting too muddy during rains.

Since my dad had a reasonably successful business, we moved into a brand new Nuuanu home. It had two stories, approximately 3,000 square feet, with a swimming pool. My dad thought of some neat things for the house. We had a built-in vacuum system (2-inch PVC system connected to a 5 horsepower vacuum). That way we didn't have to lug a vacuum cleaner around, just a 25-feet hose that plugged in to a number of outlets around the house. He also had a built-in microwave along with a regular oven. My dad thought of everything.

As I think back, it would have been natural to compare homes and family standing. Good thing I didn't! Thanks to Mom's upbringing. God didn't allow me to think highly at all of my "standing" (hey, I was just trying to graduate!). I can honestly look back and see that God was planting seeds so I would end up marrying Diana Enokawa.

HUMILITY IS EASY WHEN YOU'RE NOTHIN'!

In my early years, I wasn't "too proud." Truthfully, I hadn't accomplished anything: I never won any fights in school, except against Melvin Goto, sixth grade, when I punched him in the stomach. Nothing to celebrate; instead everyone laughed at me and said, "You punched Melvin in the stomach?"

I wasn't very good at surfing, shooting pool, ping pong, poker, bridge, or chess. Neither could I play major sports: basketball, baseball, football, or tennis. My grades were acceptable but not exceptional. But it didn't matter much since I had Diana and I spent most of my time with her.

The good thing is since I wasn't good at anything, I didn't develop a proud, arrogant attitude... until later. In fact, a week from graduating from university with a BSEE (Bachelor Science of Electrical Engineering), I thought, *What can I do after 4½ years of college?* I was not proud; in fact, I was humbled.

Of course, once I joined Dad, moved into our offices and became a Vice President, that all changed.

RISING UP CAN BE DANGEROUS TO YOUR GOD-IMAGE

In 1970, I joined my dad's company and became an instant success. I could do no wrong. Anytime I made a booboo, my dad tore into somebody else. It was his way. He probably expected that I would run the company one day, and God's Hand guided him to do two things: (1) Be sure I got correction. (2) Be sure not to break my spirit as I was just getting started.

I remember bidding a job once when my father was away on a short trip and I forgot to add the General Excise Tax. "Senior," as we called my father, (I was "Junior,") called our administrator, Robin, to his office. I was sitting at my desk but our office was small that everyone could see and hear everything as there were no partitions. He scolded Robin with the intensity of a volcano. I never ever forgot the GE tax again, but I felt compassion for Robin. My dad's logic was that Robin should have checked the bid. I didn't run my estimate by him, but I wasn't about to volunteer that information. I was too happy not to "catch HEAT"!

Anytime anyone "screwed up" on jobs, our General Foreman "Teru" got massacred. "Senior" would call in all of the foremen and scold Teru, with everyone anxiously listening. It was highly effective as everyone was enlightened, though it was Teru who got blasted. A few years ago, I attended Teru's funeral at Kalihi Union Church and found out he was a longtime Christian. I never found out if my dad's tirades helped draw him to Christ, or if being a Christian helped him endure the suffering. I guess it doesn't matter. God is always working for our good.

Since I never made a mistake, promotion to Vice President by 1972 gave me a boost. God gave me the confidence to tackle many challenging issues, projects, tasks, and responsibilities. And as I grew, Dad allowed me to "take over" parts of the operation.

"Senior" didn't have to assign me responsibility, I relished the thought of running the company. I had a crazy idea of building a mini-conglomerate of major subcontractors to negotiate projects and gain an edge in securing projects. It never would have worked but I was reading Peter Drucker's books on management and thought I knew it all. That can be dangerous to your health, wealth and even your spirit and soul, but at 28, all I could think was, "*Charge!*"

We almost went bankrupt. Twice. Once in 1978 when my dad was alive and again in 1985, after he passed. I began to question whether I knew it all.

I came up with a "Survival Plan" and raised family capital in 1986. That "plan" included Mom selling her Nuuanu dream house that Dad had built. God's perfect timing (and Plan) enabled A-1 to participate in the Japanese construction bubble of the late 80s. We made it back. Although I wasn't healed of pride and arrogance, I was at least cautious. I was now President and CEO, and the company did well.

If I learned one lesson through the 70s and 80s, it was that good times come and bad times follow. So in late 1992, I came up with a plan to deal with the tough times. It was a five-year plan, but we would budget our losses into our operational plan so we could last, and still have enough cash reserve to make it.

To "make it" means to have enough capital to keep the banks and bonding company happy. In construction, on large projects, an insurance company would need to issue the customer (normally the general contractor) a construction bond. This is a guarantee that if you failed to perform, the insurance company (bonding company) would finish the project. Also, the bank needs to extend a line of credit to provide for your cash needs.

As I maneuvered the company through the 90s, I couldn't help but think I was pretty smart. I was negotiating projects that I know would have made "Senior" proud. We also had excellent office and administrative systems, and a good field operation. We started developing a team of project engineers, estimators, project managers, and project superintendents and foremen. However, success is excellent fuel for pride and arrogance.

D-DAY

On June 6, 1993, my old man died. It was my own personal D-Day. It was also the day that I received Jesus as Lord and Savior, and it became a crucial turning point for our family, our business, and my ministry. God balanced all three areas of my life as He grew my relationship with Him.

I studied the Bible and tried to apply God's Word to how I dealt with our kids and with Diana. Although I was far from perfect, my family paradigm shifted towards God's ways. My method of dealing with family, and my attitude, changed for the better.

I began to read the Bible daily and I started volunteering. Thankfully, my First Assembly of God pastors and church had faith to allow me to participate in many areas in my early journey. I first followed Diana to the nursery then later taught Sunday classes. Pastor **Klayton Ko** allowed me to develop my own curriculum and that really helped me grow as I had the freedom to experiment. I remember teaching different topical Bible studies, then books like John, Acts, and Revelation. I also taught our men, couples, youth, and business groups as well as Assembly of God programs. It was an incredible experience. (Thank you, Pastor Ko!)

I also started ministering outside the church as God led me to **Salvation Army** (1995), **Teen Challenge** (1996), **Surfing the Nations** (1999), **Youth for Christ** (1999), as well as street evangelism. One-on-one evangelism got tough when I noticed people sweating while listening. So instead I wrote papers and produced booklets ("Christian War Package," an evangelism comic book, as well as a Japanese "War Package").

Business at A-1 was tough from 1992 through 2003, however, God blessed us. I began to believe that too was connected to God. God's Hand was with us, orchestrating the securing of many contracts. (For more, read my book, "God's Hand in the Life of an Electrician.") This helped to balance me and lower my pride and arrogance. It was always there, though, lurking in my mind.

GOD'S HAND: SURFING THE NATIONS

Since my two previous books focus a lot on **Surfing The Nations** (STN) with **Tom and Cindy Bauer**, I'll stick to a quick synopsis relevant herein.

God connected Tom and me in the late 90s through surfing and our second son, Daven. STN is a ministry that spreads the Gospel locally and internationally using surfing as a platform. They do much of their work feeding the poor and mobilizing surfers to give back. God told Tom that his ministry would take off when he reached the age of 60. In the center of Tom's heart is a big hole for the poor.

Tom once told me about helping a man who was living in a house filled with silverfish. The house was overflowing with boxes of junk, so much so that there were millions of silverfish. I thought, *What kind of guy 'loves' a stranger with a house so full of junk that silverfish took over?*

It was as if God replied, "Only a guy who has the true heart of Jesus for **all** people, especially the poor, the disadvantaged, the ones whom life has beaten down." In other words, not like you!

Tom was also a junk collector, but with a purpose: He always wanted to have a thrift store so people could come in and shop for treasure (junk). One day at STN I saw a one-ton flatbed truck filled with junk. I told Tom, "Wow, Tom, you're finally getting wise and throwing things out!" He answered: "Oh, no, we're headed to the swap meet." The swap meet was Tom's mini-church.

The people there loved him. He would set up shop, and little old ladies would come by and haggle. "How much is this?" Tom would say: "$1." "Too expensive," they came back. "I'll give you 25 cents." Tom would counter with $.50 and a deal would be struck at $.30. It wasn't the money, it was the relationships built.

God used Tom to slowly give me a heart for the poor, *the least of these.* Somehow, Isaiah 58 and Matthew 25 came alive; they weren't just words on a page, or theology. Someone really lived these passages!

It's not that there was no one else doing that. We know Mother Teresa and many other missionaries, but I never met them personally. It made a big difference to me to know Tom.

ME A PASTOR?

STN eventually lost their headquarters in Kalihi, but God was just moving them to a better place. God also was getting me ready for my final mission. All my life I thought I would live and die an electrical contractor. God had other plans.

God used STN as a stepping stone to get me connected to a Korean church called **Hawaii Cedar Church**. I eventually started teaching a Bible study at one of their ministries called the "House of Love." Through that, they asked me if I was interested in preaching on Sundays, which I did. Eventually God orchestrated events so that I would become an Assembly of God pastor. That was *HUGE!*

In a board meeting with **Aloha Ke Akua**, Reverend **Daniel Kikawa** commented that I should be a pastor. He had a 501c3 organization and could ordain me since I was already doing ministry outside the church. He mentioned that fellow board member Ken Tomita was ordained. I looked at Ken; he nodded, and God planted a thought.

I never dreamed of being a pastor. The first to suggest it was Pastor **Ernie Chow**, in the late 90s: "You ever think of becoming a pastor?" I quipped, "I can do everything I'm doing without being a pastor." People who know everything always have an answer! They don't need to pray and ask God. I didn't take him seriously, nor was I ready.

Early in 2008, a couple — Tahita and Irene — asked me to marry them. I couldn't because I wasn't a pastor, which bothered me (God was tricking me). Many people in our little church were poor and homeless, or living in public housing and shelters. It seemed like a "God idea" if they wanted to get married and change their lives for Jesus' sake, that I should be able to help them.

The thought God had planted through Rev. Kikawa took root. Daniel could ordain me based on the ministry I was already doing. Then I could marry people who wanted to take the next step. Also, I like the easy way. So at the next men's fellowship, I presented the idea to the men: Pastors **Tom Bauer** and **John Rogers**. What did they think? They were all for it, except for one small hitch: John thought I should discuss it with Pastor Ko, who was my senior pastor for the previous 13 years.

We met with Pastor Ko. He gave his blessing but mentioned another route: Assemblies of God has a Global University program for lay people, the Bereans School of the Bible. Three steps to becoming a pastor: certification, licensing, and ordainment. Once certified, you were an approved Assembly of God (AOG) pastor. I didn't feel the need, nor did I think I had the time or energy to study. It would be like going back to college!

Pastor John reached over to Pastor Ko's bookshelf and pulled out a skinny book, an older version of the course and said, "Look at this, you can probably pass without even studying." I grabbed it, like grabbing the bait, and thought, *Yeah, I could probably pass without even studying.* However, I left unconvinced.

On my way out, I stopped by Pastor Ernie Chow's office, the very person God connected me to when I accepted the Lord in 1993. I told him that I was considering being ordained under Aloha Ke Akua, but not to worry as I would remain with First Assembly of God (FAOG). My dad had come to the Lord through the outreach of Katherine Fujino while she was at FAOG's original location. As I was telling him the story, God spoke clearly to my heart: "What are you thinking? Your Dad got saved at FAOG. You got saved here. You're going to take the easy way out and just have someone ordain you? This is your home."

God knew I had to become an AOG pastor because He had plans. I started studying and in April 2010, I became a certified AOG pastor. Then God guided my steps to formalize our church.

GOD GIVES BIRTH TO CEDAR ASSEMBLY OF GOD

Hawaii Cedar Church (HCC) was a Korean church with AOG. However, there was also an English-speaking service and those attending that service were not church members. We had separate services. Eventually Cedar Assembly of God came under the covering of **General Council of the Assemblies of God**. This could not have happened if I was not an AOG pastor.

Cedar AOG and HCC had many challenges. In May 2011, Cedar AOG moved our church to Waipa Lane, where we leased facilities from All Peoples Mission Church. This was significant as we were able to secure our own sanctuary, a food pantry, thrift store, hula/Zumba rooms, showers and washer/dryer for the homeless. We also had access to areas for kitchen equipment, freezers, ice machines, and miscellaneous classrooms. Ultimately, it enabled us to expand the ministry to the poor and homeless.

However, the most significant change did not take place in operations or facilities, but in the leadership's minds and hearts. As I was studying the Bereans course, God often spoke to my heart about my journey with Him.

One significant revelation came while reading John 21: Jesus tells Peter: "Feed my sheep." I've heard this preached and read this passage dozens of times, but this time God clearly spoke to my heart. **The poor that the LORD had connected me to were Jesus' sheep.** I couldn't stop weeping upon receiving this simple revelation from God.

God moved many times in this way during my four-year journey to becoming an ordained AOG minister in April 2014. The lessons, theological background and doctrinal understanding were great, but hearing from God during my studying was "the BOMB"!

It doesn't get any simpler, and it doesn't get any better.

The next step in my journey was to welcome the congregation home. If they were Jesus' sheep, then He would want CAOG to be "home." So I started saying that this was their "home church." This was not possible under the HCC structure. However, once we had our own church, we could say that. It became obvious why God had me become a pastor, then a General Council of the Assemblies of God church.

I realized that many churches and ministries reach out to the poor and homeless. Many become members of churches after they're born again. Some know that they are only an "outreach" and have no desire to become part of the church. Unfortunately, many cannot call any church their "home church." Some do, and acclimate. But many of the poor, especially the homeless, are outreach. And they know it.

However, God was not satisfied: being a "home church" to some. Next, He had us call the church "our family," and we tried our best to live that out. Our concept is to live life together, so we meet Sundays, Tuesdays and Wednesdays. (Our Core Group also meets every other Friday for teaching and training.) **This concept of family**, and the discipleship that goes with it, **is now the core focus of our church**.

Our Mission Statement reads: "To bring Jesus Christ into our homes and to the people of Honolulu and Hawaii, and with Jesus as part of their lives, help them to become self-sustaining, reunite the families, and have their children become leaders of tomorrow." Our vision for 2020 is "To see all the poor transformed by the Holy Spirit into a powerful life-giving force."

I'll be the first to say we have a long way to go. Having a great mission and vision statement does not make the challenge any easier. God has His work cut out for us, and He has to show up for any lasting, long-term impact.

CAN WE CHANGE THE POOR?

Diana and I have had a very interesting, rewarding, and challenging journey over the past few years at Cedar Assembly of God. We've met many different people but they all fall into four different categories:

First, the **poor who don't want to change**. Many Biblical truths explain why people would rather remain in their condition than be transformed. These include bad habits, laziness, and fear (which is just an excuse for laziness as in Proverbs 22:13 about a supposed lion that preempts action).

Second, **some *want* to change, but don't want to pay the price, put in the effort, or take the necessary risk to make the change.**

Third, some **want to change but are satisfied with a minimal level of transformation** that gets them to an acceptable lifestyle. It's not much but they convince themselves that they don't want more — either spiritually of God, materially in wealth, emotionally in stability, or motivationally in effort. They put in minimal effort to reach this lifestyle, and once they reach it, they stop.

Fourth, many (if not most) **love Jesus and grow from the beginning**. They have been to many outreaches, and have attended many different churches over their lives. They have attended Catholic churches, Assembly of God churches, Foursquare churches, Salvation Army services, and many more. Most of these have made multiple professions of faith and have already given their lives to Jesus prior to coming to CAOG. Theirs is a living testament of which Paul wrote, *"neither he who plants nor he who waters is anything, but **only God, who makes things grow***" (1 Corinthians 3:7, emphasis added). They are hungry and make me, as a pastor, look good. Thank you, Body of Christ, for doing the advance work.

People in the first three categories usually stop coming to church, stop reading their Bibles, and stop building relationships. Some slowly but surely fall back into the same lifestyle and crash. Many of these fall into the first three groups that Jesus illustrated in the 'Parable of the Sower' (Mt. 13):

1. Satan snatches away whatever is sown in their hearts and they are blinded to the truth and to their condition.
2. Some hear the Word, receive it with joy, but have no foundation. So they last only a short time and then fall away.
3. Some receive the Word but have so many other concerns that the Word cannot penetrate the soul and grow.
4. The fourth type are ones who find Jesus and hear clearly the Gospel that Jesus wants to make a difference in their lives and the lives of their family and friends. When these grow into strong Christians, they eventually want to reach out to those they barely know and even to their enemies.

This group matches Jesus' fourth group who produce thirty, sixty or a hundred times what was sown. They are the one who hear the Word, understand and produce an abundant crop.

What makes ministry difficult is knowing that many in the fourth group will still struggle all of their lives. They love God, but are still homeless. It's not that they don't want to work, many cannot for reasons most of us will never comprehend.

One of my early sermons struck such a note. Our congregation is like any typical Pentecostal church: They laugh and shout at the right time without interrupting. And they sing, loud! Many enjoy the worship more than my message. My own son Daven says, "Dad, sometimes your messages are hard to follow." I thrive on their feedback and responses. However, this one message was on becoming self-sustaining, how the skilled worker will serve kings; and if you don't work, you don't eat. The hush was deafening. I had to retool.

HEARING FROM GOD THROUGH PASTOR DARRICK

Pastor Darrick (PD) and I were talking about one of our longtime attendees, Daryl, whom we both love. Daryl is homeless, as is all of his family. They number close to ten in four different families. Daryl gets high when he has money. Many usually disappear the first week of the month when they get their blessing from the state. PD said: "When he gets saved, then what?"

PD wasn't talking smack about Daryl; he was talking about real life, Daryl as an example. He has no skills, weak habits, low motivation, and huge health issues. Yet he's a survivor. They move their tents from tree to sidewalk to tree, depending on which way the wind is blowing. Daryl probably is saved, so PD was asking a rhetorical question.

"Then what?"

Is that it? Is that the end? We try to get them saved, feed them a little (very little). If all churches feed them a little, and that ends up to be a lot, is God pleased? Is that it?

Those who are truly saved are new creations but how does God *"cause everything to work together for the good of those who love God..."*? Especially when they're homeless, in public housing, the middle class headed to poverty, the college kid with no job, and the elderly who are dying?

Are these fair questions?

I am not going through a mid-life Christian crisis. I am following Peter Drucker's model of finding out God's heart by asking questions. I'm on a journey not just to live 10 or 20 more years, but to know God, His thoughts and desires, His movement, His passion, and, along with these, my mission. If you decide to journey with me, you might clarify your mission too. That would be cool.

LIVING LIFE TOGETHER

"They devoted themselves to the apostles' teaching and to the
fellowship, to the breaking of bread and to prayer.
Everyone was filled with awe, and many wonders and miraculous signs
were done by the apostles.
All the believers were together and had everything in common.
Selling their possessions and goods, they gave to anyone as he had need.
Every day they continued to meet together in the temple courts.
They broke bread in their homes and ate together with glad and sincere
hearts, praising God and enjoying the favor of all the people.
And the Lord added to their number daily those who were being saved."
(Acts 2:42-47)

This anchor verse is our model at CAOG. We call it, "Living life together." We meet three times each week (our servers meet more), and we have teaching, fellowship, food, movie and game days, showers, and prayer. We desire to see transformation in our congregation, but do not have unreasonable expectations that "We must do it."

We also have a lot of very challenging situations:
* Police show up once in awhile…
* Person pulls a knife because they felt threatened by a person who attacked them with an umbrella…
* Person pulls a knife on someone for making fun of him because of the mess he made in the showers…
* Person breaks his ukulele on the head of the person who threatened his friend with a knife. (He waited till he was off the property so he thought it was okay. We banned him for one month. We do it in love.)…
* Person beats his girlfriend (blood flows) because she was upset and yelling at another girl who was braiding his hair. He is banned, and then he threatens to come back and shoot Pastor Darrick and everyone…
* Person comes and is looking for someone who owes him money…
* Person comes looking for someone who he claimed raped his wife, while he was staying with them…
* Person stabs someone at 2:30 am and I see his picture in the paper. He says it wasn't his fault. It never is…but this time I believe him…
* There are many "incidents" because people complain about others, because of something done or not done.

We have excellent security teams. They have the authority to ban people for a day, a week, a month, even six months if they don't stop what they are doing. Security also may call 911 if things get out of hand. God protects us and the police usually come within minutes.

Yet living life together is our model and all are welcomed back when the ban ends. We trust God each day.

PEOPLE WHO CANNOT SEE, CANNOT SEE

Jesus taught: *"Though seeing, they do not see; though hearing, they do not hear,"* (Matthew 13:13). No sense using toothpicks to hold eyes open. We can't change hearts with toothpicks. Only God can open eyes. Jesus explains, *"But blessed are your eyes because they see, and your ears because they hear,"* (Matthew 13:16-17).

Jesus tells us some receive because their hearts are open. Some have major turmoil which makes receiving difficult, and so they are unfruitful in their Christian walk. Some have issues for which their paradigm of life doesn't allow the Gospel to firmly take root in their lives and they fall away. Others have been blinded by their paradigm of life and they are never truly born again.

It is difficult to discern the types of people and the stages of life they are in. Many are fine in church, but after church and outside in the real world is another story. Our dependence is on our Lord:

God can draw them.

God can convict them.

God can have them go through rough times and the Gospel immediately makes sense as they call out to Jesus.

It appears to me that the people who can see, truly see. Those that cannot see, cannot. As I apply this truth to those at Cedar AOG, **I begin to realize that I really cannot make much impact to the poor. It is the work of God, entirely.** That does not mean I will not give it my best, my all. But it helps me refocus on my goal: God is working for my good so I can become like His Son. **Success is what happens within me, as I walk the journey. Success is not having a perfect congregation.**

GOD'S MODEL: LIVE LIFE TOGETHER

I am not trying to live like the farmer who shoots an arrow on the side of his barn, and then draws a bulls-eye around the arrow. I am not giving myself a goal that will automatically bring success. But I am looking for truth properly applied to the mission and ministry God has given us (Diana, along with my leadership team). This will help us develop our programs and doctrinal application.

I recognize that God has called us to this ministry, and we intend to continue as long as God keeps us here. We've discovered that many who come have lifelong issues that are cultural, family-related, or emotional and go back all of their lives. It's easy to teach that they are new creations, but in reality, **change is really slow**.

There are always situations that arise where their paradigm is such that the immediate and automatic reaction takes them back to square one, and we see the wretched man they are. Our philosophy has been, that we are family, and no matter what, even if we have to ban someone for a season, we always welcome them back.

Our goal is not success as defined by no failures or outbursts, but success in humbling oneself to come back and start again. Our goal is to become like Jesus. We do not teach our congregation to shoot for perfection defined by never blowing up or getting angry; but when the inevitable happens, to say "Sorry," or, "I forgive you."

So our model is to "Live life together as a family."

Our goal at CAOG is to create the best environment where the family — whether members, key leaders, the wannabe members, or the crowd — can come together and duplicate the book of Acts.

We hope that our people feel at home, feel loved, and feel that this is the best place to be during the days that we are here. We hope that if they are banned (a disciplinary process for violent, threatening behavior), that they miss home and can hardly wait to return. We have seen this happen.

However the optimum target is still inner, godly growth in having Jesus bring life, and recognizing that He is enough for life and godliness.

THE BRADY GIUSTA MODEL

One day I got a call from one of our early pastors, Pastor **Paul Tomonari**. He told me about a guy he had met who was ministering at Farrington High School, **Brady Giusta**. We invited Brady to one of our monthly "**Kalihi Unite**" meetings. It was a loose group of like-minded people in Kalihi who wanted to make a difference. We had pastors, businessmen, lay people from churches, friends, anyone who loved Kalihi, fellowship and food.

A few months later, we were looking for someone for our youth ministry. God reminded me about Brady and I asked him if anyone was interested. He suggested Evander, and God solidified our relationship at the same time.

Brady had an interesting story: He was heavy into drugs, mainly marijuana, and making a lot of money. Eventually God drew him to a YoungLife camp and he laid a fleece for God as his own life hung literally in the balance. He was up a tree, on a high branch about 60-80 feet up, ready to end his life. He wanted a sign from God that He was real. God sent a flock of birds to Brady. His life turned around and hasn't been the same since.

Brady (figure 1, page 91) got involved in YoungLife, whose model is to live life with the kids to whom they minister. They operate primarily with volunteers (approximately 50 at this writing). The volunteers pledge to devote 10 hours a week to living life with the high school and middle school kids. They have Friday after-school meetings, and they spend time playing basketball, football, surfing, eating, and just hanging out.

The picture that came while listening to Brady was a football team. Most members on a high school team play very little, some not at all. Yet they go to practice every day during season. They run, do pushups, lift weights, sweat, bleed, and work to exhaustion. Why do they do it? How do they continue, day after day? Simple, they are part of the team.

It hit me: **Cedar AOG needs to be part of a team. Cedar AOG needs to be part of a family.**

We thought we were doing it, but not really. Instead, we were doing church.

I realized the problem was with me. I knew the people were Jesus' sheep, and wept when God whacked me with that revelation. Our congregation would even say, "This is our 'home church.'" But it wasn't enough.

Now we are a family. Albeit, a church family, different from a person's blood family, but as close as a *hanai* (adopted) family. Something changed in my heart when I called my congregation my "family."

So our model is to live life together as best we can, loving each other, encouraging each other, supporting each other, challenging each other; fighting and making up like any normal family.

GOD HAS A PLAN FOR AMERICA

GOD LOVES THE POOR

I have been blessed these past few years knowing that God was training me all along through schooling, as an electrical contractor, then drawing me to First Assembly of God, so He could bring me to Jesus and my ultimate call as a pastor. He built a church consisting of the poor, knowing that the journey that He had me on would humble me and help me become more like His Son.

God created me as a dreamer and I always had big dreams. That was bad early on and resulted in brushes with bankruptcy; yet God created me this way for the journey and mission that He had planned for me. My dream was to be the biggest electrical contractor, a mini-conglomerate of subcontractors. God knew those crazy dreams would keep me striving to learn, grow, improve, have a "never give up" attitude. These big dreams were fueled by a little alcohol and marijuana in my early years.

God protected me while I was stoned, drunk or loaded. His Hand guided me and saved me when one crash could have taken me out or crippled me for life. I may have even ended up homeless.

God also knew He would use those memories to express His love for me, once I saw the light. They would help my relationship with His Son develop and grow so that I would be pliable in His Hands.

God gave me a deep affinity for the poor through my experiences. He also showed me clearly that from which He had to deliver me. Everything I have today and everything I am now is a blessing beyond comprehension — husband, father, CEO, friend, and pastor. All of it is due to His plan and His Hand (Is. 26:12).

GOD LOVES AMERICA

As I think about the poor, my thoughts cannot help but turn upward to God: *What is He thinking? Why are so many poor? Is He trying to tell us something about the poor in America? If God loves us and is working for our good, why is this happening? How did we get here? Isn't America the greatest nation on earth? Then where are the George Washingtons and Abraham Lincolns of today?*

I seek answers to questions that seem to have no answers, yet I realize I won't get anywhere unless I start looking at America as a nation. Then we'll investigate God's thinking: What is He up to? We'll conclude by identifying our global mission. No pressure.☺

Join me and have fun.

CHAPTER 2

AMERICA THE BUSTED

"I sought for the greatness and genius of America
in her commodious harbors and her ample
rivers – and it was not there...
in her fertile fields and boundless forests and it was not there...
in her rich mines and her vast world
commerce – and it was not there...
in her democratic Congress and her matchless Constitution
– and it was not there.
Not until I went into the churches of America and heard her pulpits
aflame with righteousness
did I understand the secret of her genius and power.
America is great because she is good, and if America ever ceases
to be good, she will cease to be great."
AUTHOR UNKNOWN

This indictment of the greatness and downfall of America is confirmed by the Bible:

> **"Those who obey God will be blessed; those who do**
> **not obey will be cursed by God"** (Deut. 28).

America was great because she obeyed and pleased God. Then America moved away from God and disobeyed Him; she no longer worships Him. Consequently, America is busted and bankrupt.

I love America, vote, pay taxes, do jury duty, obey traffic laws (maybe a little speeding), do not jaywalk (I cannot afford the ticket!), and love our pledge of liberty and justice for all.

But America is broken and broke.

YOUNG DREAMS CAN SPELL T-R-O-U-B-L-E

Dreams can inspire us to study hard, be disciplined, and never give up. God gives dreams and He uses them to help us keep pressing forward in life. My big dreams got me into trouble. I never analyzed the risk of large projects nor the downside of loss. When you're young, you never consider the cost.

As I look back, I realize the problem was not actually the dream; it was success and power. When I became a Vice President, pride crept in. A-1 was doing well and I thought I had a lot to do with it prospering. It never occured to me that it may be my Dad's war experience which kept him humble, his 30 years as an electrician, and his 20 years growing his business and staff. I thought it was my managerial skills, our job costing system, or our new computer system. Most of all, I thought I was the greatest. But God was working.

The Bible gives only two men and one woman who handled success and promotion well: **Joseph**, **Samuel**, and **Esther**. All the kings of Israel failed miserably the test of pride and became arrogant, which led to their fall. The kings of Judah fared better but still had bouts of pride. However, a few heeded God's correction and returned to Him; good examples include **King David** and **Hezekiah**.

So it is with America today.

AMERICA'S DREAMS LED BY CARNAL DESIRES

Americans have great, God-given natural resources, an industrious people, a Constitution that gave all peoples an opportunity for a better life and our children an unlimited future. Americans have gone through two world wars and came out on top of the world.

Our economy was refined by God and robust by the 20s, 30s, and 40s. In fact it was the GREATEST economy ever. As long as America had our head and heart in the right place, we were a nation concerned with other nations. Our very citizens came from those nations. We prospered.

Then something happened.

Americans began thinking, **We are the greatest!** America became proud of her accomplishments, forgetting God. We pushed God from our lives and our culture. It started a slippery slope that lead quickly to national demise. In 1962, the Supreme Court removed prayer from schools. In 1973 we legalized the killing of babies in abortion.

God may be thinking: *First you eject me from schools, then you approve the killing of babies. You give it a name, and you pass laws approving it. Don't look for my blessing. I removed it from America.*

How is abortion different from Israel sacrificing babies in the fire to the god Molech?

Some argue that it was only a few that allowed this. God may answer: **And it only takes a few with power in key areas**. Power grows in the hands of a few when the wrong they do goes unchecked. God helped create a Constitution with checks and balances. The judges were to hold their office as long as they showed "*good Behavior*":

Article III of the Constitution

"Section 1. The judicial Power of the United States, shall be vested in one supreme Court, and in such inferior Courts as the Congress may from time to time ordain and establish. The Judges, both of the supreme and inferior Courts, shall hold their Offices during **good Behavior**, and shall, at stated Times, receive for their Services a Compensation, which shall not be diminished during their Continuance in Office."

Granted, the legal issues behind Roe vs. Wade as with its companion Doe vs. Bolton are complex. The initial intent of the court trying to balance the 9th Amendment and 14th Amendment rights of women and give them the right to an abortion have long ago fallen by the wayside. Americans wanted this. It's all about "freedom." We wanted the freedom to have sex with whoever we wanted. Soon after abandoning our Judeo-Christian roots, America's decline was sealed.

Similarly, the downfall of Israel started as soon as they left Egypt. We see glimpses with Samuel's kids: Joel and Abijah who *"turned aside after dishonest gain and accepted bribes and perverted justice"* (1 Sam. 8:3).

King David loved God and was a man after God's heart. David's son, Solomon, lost his way. Solomon's son, Rehoboam, rejected God's ways. And then after the very next generation, everything crashed.

It only takes a few. But if those "few" are leaders, the nation turns to the same wickedness. God was patient with Israel and sent many prophets to get the nation to turn back to Him. They didn't.

AMERICA IS BROKEN

In America, the Supreme Court has led our system to become broken. And under this broken system, people no longer trust or approve of Congress or our President.

The American dream is now a nightmare. We all know that. What we don't know is **WHY?** How did we get here? Is there a way out? Is there a fix?

The checks and balances built into the Constitution are long gone. The rich and powerful heavily influence the elections of the President and Congress; local rich and influential power brokers do the same in State and City elections. The mantra is **no longer "we the people"; it is "we the powerful."**

IS GOD SURPRISED? IS HE IN CONTROL?

What if God has a different goal for us?

What if working to "fix" the system is not the end goal? (This does not mean we don't try, it's simply accepting that God is Sovereign.)

What if those who work only to fix the system will become broken in the long run?

What if God has given America (and the world) all the rope it needs to destroy itself, economically, financially, and socially so that:

1. He can bring discipline on America.
2. During the time of discipline, people will fall on their knees and cry out to God.
3. When the people cry out and change their ways, He will heal the land.

Biblical basis:

(Isaiah 46:10-11)

"I make known the end from the beginning, from ancient times, what is still to come. I say: My purpose will stand, and I will do all that I please. From the east I summon a bird of prey; from a far-off land, a man to fulfill my purpose. What I have said, that will I bring about; what I have planned, that will I do."

(Hosea 5:10, 14-15)

"Judah's leaders are like those who move boundary stones. I will pour out my wrath on them like a flood of water.... For I will be like a lion to Ephraim, like a great lion to Judah. I will tear them to pieces and go away;

I will carry them off, with no one to rescue them. Then I will go back to my place until they admit their guilt. And they will seek my face; in their misery they will earnestly seek me."

(2 Chronicles 7:14-15)

"...If my people, who are called by my name, will humble themselves and pray and seek my face and turn from their wicked ways, then will I hear from heaven and will forgive their sin and will heal their land."

If this is the case, **is all hope lost? Does this mean we do nothing?**

Definitely not:

1. We should always do what we believe God is calling us to do, yet trust Him for the ultimate good that only **He** can work out in our lives.
2. We are not to be results-oriented, but **faith-oriented**, recognizing God is sovereign and continuing to seek after what He is doing in our world.
3. We can then follow Him, hear from Him, suffer along with the world for the sake of the salvation of others, who will surely be watching us. Suffering is the best builder of hope and love (Rom. 5:3-5).

AMERICAN ABANDONED GOD, SO GOD HAS ABANDONED AMERICA DECLARATION OF INDEPENDENCE — HOW WE HAVE STRAYED

The Declaration of Independence is one of our foundational documents:

"When in the Course of human events, it becomes necessary for one people to dissolve the political bands which have connected them with another, and to assume among the powers of the earth, the separate and equal station to which the

Laws of Nature and of Nature's God entitle them, a decent respect to the opinions of mankind requires that they should declare the causes which impel them to the separation.

We hold these truths to be self-evident, that all men are created equal, that they are **endowed by their Creator with certain unalienable Rights**, that among these are Life, Liberty and the pursuit of Happiness. That to secure these rights, Governments are **instituted among Men, deriving their just powers from the consent of the governed....**"

Our Founding Fathers recognized America's blessings and rights came from God. These blessings are bestowed only as long as Americans obey God's Laws: "...To which the **Laws of Nature and of Nature's God entitle them**...."

When we don't follow God's ways, these blessings and "certain unalienable Rights...Life, Liberty and the pursuit of Happiness..." are withdrawn by God. God has given America, through her Constitution, a responsibility. We have **disregarded that responsibility**.

The last phrase "Governments are instituted among Men, **deriving their just powers from the consent of the governed**..." is **no longer true in America**. Elected politicians have figured out a way around having the people elect the best person that will protect their God-given rights. They've structured laws so big business interests will funnel money to those candidates that pass laws that give them the advantage for huge profits. They circumvent the truth with words. We used to call that deception, but now since everyone is doing it, it is all about perception. And "perception is reality." (figure 2, page 92)

People know that elected politicians don't listen, so they've **given up their voting rights and not participated in elections**. As such, elected officials do not "**deriv[e] just powers from the consent of the governed**."

That in a nutshell is the reason our nation is "busted."

The Christians have not done what our God desires. God brought the pilgrims to America. He orchestrated our fight for freedom to throw off the yoke from England:

> "When in the Course of human events, it becomes necessary for one people to dissolve the political bands which have connected them with another...."

God gave us the right to select our government officials and bureaucracy. When we abandon that right, we disobey God. We have allowed fools to be elected. And when they come into power, who do they naturally select for their bureaucracy? "If a ruler listens to lies, all his officials become wicked" (Prov. 29:12). Further, "Those who forsake the law praise the wicked, but those who keep the law resist them" (Prov. 28:4). "Evil men do not understand justice, but those who seek the LORD understand it fully" (Prov. 28:5).

God will hold Christians responsible. We cannot disregard our responsibility to elect Godly men of integrity (Ex. 18), then sit around and complain about laws and policies. God will not overlook our laziness. We will be disciplined, like any father would a disobedient child.

One influential arena is American politics. There is a movement of God's Hand sweeping across Hawaii and the rest of the United States: Christians have not been involved in politics. I won't guess why. However, our focus is on what we can do now: this movement is **Christians getting back on track and involved in American politics, as a foundational responsibility from our Founding Fathers**.

Politics has become a nasty word. Politicians are "fools" themselves or have been influenced/controlled by "fools." And by "fools," I'm not using Webster's definition but the **Bible. Let's take a look.**

THE BUREAUCRACY: WHAT'S WRONG?

The bureaucracy is a body of non-elected government officials and/ or administrative policymaking group. According to Wikipedia, a bureaucracy "refers to the administrative system governing any large institution."

The bureaucracy is ineffective in advancing the cause of the people and caring for the very constituents for whom they work. According to God's Word, the reason God **"frustrates"** world systems, causing confusion within them, is to render them ineffective. They may still make money, but those whose focus is profit and money will end up in a God-orchestrated disaster.

In fact, God is allowing the bureaucracy to be occupied by people He calls "fools." He *"frustrates"* their efforts so that it will be impossible for these "fools" to run global organizations. Author Peter Drucker says **profit cannot be the motive**; a business has a social responsibility to care for people, whom he calls "our greatest assets." As such, one foundational goal in any successful enterprise is to create the **"achieving worker."**

> *"There is an evil I have seen under the sun, the sort of error that arises from a ruler: Fools are put in many high positions, while the rich occupy the low ones."* (Ecclesiastes 10:5-6)

My intention is not to disrespect people in government. I also certainly do not think they're uneducated. Elected officials and appointed civil servants are typically college-educated, many with advanced degrees. They're highly educated, highly skilled and talented.

However, they are deficient in one key area which renders them fools: **They have no relationship with God**. In fact, many do not believe in God; or believe in multiple gods; or are deists, believing an impersonal God created the universe then went on a long vacation.

Some stretch the truth or simply tell outright lies. Some go after dishonest gain. After awhile, all chase after the same.

All their education, skill and talent do not make up for wisdom from God:

> "For it is written: 'I will destroy the **wisdom of the wise**; the intelligence of the intelligent **I will frustrate**.' Where is the wise man? Where is the scholar? Where is the philosopher of this age? Has not **God made foolish the wisdom of the world**? Brothers, think of what you were when you were called. Not many of you were wise by human standards; not many were influential; not many were of noble birth. But God chose the foolish things of the world to shame the wise; God chose the weak things of the world to shame the strong...." (1 Corinthians 1:19-31)

Applied to today's troubles, God is telling us He will cause governments who turn from Him to be **"frustrated."** Ultimately, their programs will not work. The monetary system of our government and the Federal Reserve will fail. Government and business attempts to profit will work short-term (decades are short in God's timeframe), but will eventually cause long-term economic turmoil that will incur world pain. Social programs — Social Security, Medicaid, Medicare, ObamaCare — will eventually fail and cause huge economic dislocation. We already see this happening in Europe's economies.

Yet in spite of all of this, God's people who stand strong in faith and continue to do what He has calls us to do, will not only survive but thrive because we know there is no failure: **We will win!** We have eternal life. We have abundant life. We know God loves us and we love God. God is always with us. He will never leave us. There was never a time that God did not love us. We can never die.

We love others as He loves us, and we go into the world to make a difference in people's lives by sharing the Good News. When we,

Christians called by His name, do as He tells us to, God puts rich-and-talented, bureaucratic "fools" to shame. By using lowly, humble Christians living a godly life.

WHAT IS GOD'S DEFINITION OF A "FOOL"?

"The fool says in his heart, 'There is no God.' They are corrupt, their deeds are vile; there is no one who does good." (Psalms 14:1)

"A fool finds pleasure in evil conduct, but a man of understanding delights in wisdom." (Proverbs 10:23)

"The way of a fool seems right to him, but a wise man listens to advice." (Proverbs 12:15)

"A fool finds no pleasure in understanding but delights in airing his own opinions." (Proverbs 18:2)

"As a dog returns to its vomit, so a fool repeats his folly." (Proverbs 26:11)

"The wise man has eyes in his head, while the fool walks in the darkness…." (Ecclesiastes 2:14)

"Extortion turns a wise man into a fool, and a bribe corrupts the heart." (Ecclesiastes 7:7)

"For the fool speaks folly, his mind is busy with evil: He practices ungodliness and spreads error concerning the Lord; the hungry he leaves empty and from the thirsty he withholds water." (Isaiah 32:6)

God tells us how fools live and act. God also tells us that fools have no excuse for not recognizing Him:

"The wrath of God is being revealed from heaven against all the godlessness and wickedness of men who suppress the truth by their wickedness, since what may be known about God is plain to them, **because God has made it plain to them.** *For since the creation of the world God's invisible qualities —* **his eternal power and divine nature** *— have been* **clearly seen, being understood from what has been made, so that men are without excuse.***"
(Romans 1:18-20)

Fools cannot claim innocence or ignorance for God makes it *"plain"* to them!

FOOLS ARE IN CONTROL

"There is an evil I have seen under the sun, the sort of error that arises from a ruler: Fools are put in many high positions, while the rich occupy the low ones." (Ecclesiastes 10:5-6)

Based on God's definition of fools, it's obvious there are many fools in control within all branches of Federal, State and Local Government. Sure, many Christians serve in these areas, so by God's definition, they are not fools. But they are not in control. Their voices are not heard and they are outvoted, outgunned, or outmaneuvered. Or they are afraid of retribution. I am not referring to these Christians. Even in political circles, they go along and wait for the right time to make a small difference; hence they are unable to make a major impact for God. Christians everywhere have been effectively silenced by the "Intolerance" doctrine prevalent in America and our World: You're intolerant if you cannot tolerate evil.

Of course, I am also not referring to the Christian businessperson. These key community influencers sometimes bend the ear of bureaucrats to impact God's Kingdom through wise godly counsel. Examples would include **Joseph**, **Esther** and **Daniel**. But these are exceptions, not norms.

WHERE GOD'S DEFINITION OF "FOOLS" REIGN:

1. Liberal News Media
2. Liberal Hollywood
3. Federal, State & Local Government (including both Executive and Legislative)
4. Judicial System (many judges are appointed by fools; fools appoint fools). They are legislating from the bench and creating case laws that govern our system today.
5. Central Banking System — The Federal Reserve is out of control in creating money. Fools are at the helm, as they are appointed by fools.
6. Commercial Banking System
7. Financial Banking System
8. Big Business — seeks profit at expense of people and long-term corporate survival. The profit they make today, enables "big guns" to take big bonuses. This concept violates one of Peter Drucker's most important concepts: "People are our greatest assets."

One clear example of fools in big business: the Veterans Affairs (V.A.) scandal. The V.A. bureaucracy deliberately falsified waiting list times so that they met performance goals and got their bonuses. Meanwhile, unfortunately, our American veterans suffered and even died. And by the number of incidents reported, these widespread "lies" have been going on for some time. Again, at the expense of the very people that bureaucracy was designed to serve.

"Dr. Jacqueline Brecht, a former urologist at the Alaska V.A. Healthcare System in Anchorage, said in an interview that she had a heated argument with administrators at a staff meeting in 2008 when she objected to using phantom appointments to make wait times appear shorter, as they had instructed her. She said the practice amounted to **medical fraud**....

35

"Days later a top administrator came to Brecht's clinic, put her on administrative leave and had security walk her out of the building.

'It's scary to think that people can try to stand up and do the right thing, and this is the reaction,' said Brecht, now in private practice in Massachusetts.

Her complaints were corroborated by other Alaska personnel and were the subject of an email that Brecht sent to a military doctor at the time. Brecht wrote that administrators 'schedule fake patient appointments' [i.e. commit FRAUD]. She wrote: 'They do so just so our numbers look good to D.C.'"
(*NY Times*, Eric Lichblau, article printed Honolulu Star-Advertiser, 6/16/14, page 1)

God is working against these fools to "*frustrate*" their efforts. But the beat goes on, and on, and on. Administrators kick the can down the road and problems are unresolved; they just get larger and larger and larger.

One day, God will pull the rug out from one part of these interconnected systems, and the entire system will collapse.

When? It is unknowable.

Can it be solved? It is unsolvable.

Can it be prevented? It is unpreventable. The systems are bucking against God.

Everyone will be affected: "*He causes his sun to rise on the evil and the good, and sends rain on the righteous and the unrighteous*" (Mt. 5:45-46). However, it will be a test for Christians: Will we stand strong? Will our love grow cold?

FOOLS MISINTERPRET THE CONSTITUTION

"*The way of a fool seems right to him.*" (Proverbs 12:15)

The First Amendment was intended to protect the people from Government. The Government has misinterpreted a letter that Thomas Jefferson wrote to the Danbury Baptist Association:

"To Messrs. Nehemiah Dodge and Others, a Committee of the Danbury Baptist Association, in the State of Connecticut
"Gentleman,

"The affectionate sentiments of esteem and approbation which you are so good as to express towards me, on behalf of the Danbury Baptist Association, give me the highest satisfaction. My duties dictate a faithful and zealous pursuit of the interests of my constituents, and in proportion as they are persuaded of my fidelity to those duties, the discharge of them becomes more and more pleasing.

Believing with you that religion is a matter which lies solely between man and his God, that he owes account to none other for his faith or his worship, that the legislative powers of government reach actions only, and not opinions, I contemplate with sovereign reverence that act of the whole American people which declared that **their legislature should make no law respecting an establishment of religion, or prohibiting the free exercise thereof thus building a wall of separation between church and State.** Adhering to this expression of the supreme will of the nation in behalf of the rights of conscience, I shall see with sincere satisfaction the progress of those sentiments which tend to restore to man all his natural rights, convinced he has no natural right in opposition to his social duties.

I reciprocate your kind prayers for the protection and blessing of the common Father and Creator of man, and tender you for yourselves and your religious association, assurances of my high respect and esteem.

Th. Jefferson

January 1, 1802

Thomas Jefferson essentially quotes the First Amendment of the Constitution which says:

"Congress shall make no law respecting an establishment of religion, or prohibiting the free exercise thereof; or abridging the freedom of speech, or of the press; or the right of the people peaceably to assemble, and to petition the Government for a redress of grievances."

The Constitution was protecting the people from Government, not wanting Government to establish a universal church over America. They did not want another England here, which is why they broke free from its rule and authority.

The Supreme Court used that very same letter of Thomas Jefferson's to remove prayer from school.

The fools on the bench (the Warren Supreme Court, 1963, eight out of nine justices) have effectively rewritten the Constitution. This is now law that opened the flood of "separation of church and state." They effectively established a new paradigm from which other laws build their foundation. Therefore, America's laws in this area are built on a faulty foundation, and God must do something.

But the "fools" are not to blame. "We the people" are responsible because we didn't rise up. We had the Constitution to remove the "fools," but didn't. We should have impeached the judges who made the decision to remove prayer from the schools. Now, change can only be made with God; and He is moving.

U.S. Constitution Article III

"Section 1. The judicial Power of the United States, shall be vested in one supreme Court, and in such inferior Courts as the Congress may from time to time ordain and establish. The Judges, both of the supreme and inferior Courts, shall hold their

Offices **during good Behavior,** and shall, at stated Times, receive for their Services a Compensation, which shall not be diminished during their Continuance in Office."

First the "fools" took prayer out of school using their own twisted logic from Jefferson; then they authorized abortion (killing babies) ten years later. An America that cannot see that this violates every semblance of "good behavior" does not deserve God to watch over it.

Now it will take much longer for us to right our course. I'm not sure God will wait that long. And He will hold Christians accountable. He gave Christians the responsibility to shine the light of truth to the nation. **We have done a poor job, so God will make us poor.**

GOVERNMENT NOT CARING FOR AMERICA
HEARING FROM GOD IS NOT EASY

Jesus taught: *"Love the Lord your God with all your heart and with all your soul and with all your mind. This is the first and greatest commandment. And the second is like it: 'Love your neighbor as yourself'"* (Matthew 22:37-39).

God establishes a principle: (Deut. 28:1-6)

1. If you fully obey the Lord your God and carefully follow all His commands today, the Lord your God will set you high above all the nations on earth.
2. All [the following] blessings will come upon you if you obey the Lord your God.
3. You will be blessed in the city and blessed in the country.
4. The fruit of your womb will be blessed, and the crops of your land and the young of your livestock — the calves of your herds and the lambs of your flocks.
5. Your basket and your kneading trough will be blessed.
6. You will be blessed when you come in and blessed when you go out.

Christians' blessings do not depend on government and how well it performs. Our ultimate blessing comes from knowing Jesus, loving God, and obeying Him. We pray we get to that place; meanwhile, we know that between now and the time we see Jesus face-to-face there will be many bumps.

Obedience is easily preached, not easily lived. Often I think I'm obeying God, then Diana tells me something and I'm thrown off. Sure, I believe God speaks through wives, but only 10% of the time. My challenge is knowing which 10%.

So what I try to do is listen to her 100% of the time; then I'll be *sure* to catch all that God is saying. That's not always easy because I'm typically already moving forward on an assignment when she speaks direction. My "personal prophet" has the power to redirect my focus mid-mission and can even drown out God's voice; I must discern wisely.

We all have hundreds of assignments — as fathers, husbands, brothers, pastors, businesspeople, friends, church ministry leaders, all while providing for our families. Wives have complementary responsibilities. As I think about America's course correction today, the picture I get is one of an ant jumping on the back of a charging elephant and trying to get him to change course.

We have one advantage over the ant: **nothing is impossible with God**. Therefore, if God set up America with a Constitution by which He is guiding us and determining our ultimate blessing, we would be wise to obey. First, we need to know what He might desire from the Constitution. Also, we don't need to do everything all at once. We will all have different roles, depending on the gifts, talents, and resources He gave each of us.

The Bible is our main guide plus we must also hear directly from the Lord. God tells us to obey our authorities since He allowed all authority. And because one authority structure is our Constitution, let's take a look at the connection between the Constitution and the Bible.

WHAT DOES THE CONSTITUTION HAVE TO DO WITH GOD?

There is no question America has been blessed by God. It has great and fertile lands, abundant rain, rivers, natural resources, and, most importantly, a **united people**. That blessing is directly connected to Creator God and the Founding Fathers recognized this. In recognizing the Creator, they also recognized and lived in a deep relationship with Him. They realized God gave them the responsibility and the wisdom to craft a Constitution that would result in people uniting to form the United States of America.

The Constitution and Bill of Rights ensured that Government knew they were accountable to the people, and were to put the people first. Laws enacted by Government allowed all people access to rights bestowed by the Creator: *"life, liberty, and pursuit of happiness."* People from different lands, cultures, languages, religions, sex and belief systems came together, worked and lived together because our Constitution and laws of the land allowed free markets, free speech, and religious rights for all. All could worship God freely; it is God's way, free will.

Entrepreneurs and workers alike could build business, become homeowners, property owners, raise a family. Their children had equal opportunity for a better future and had unlimited opportunity. Industrious workers had freedom to start and build new businesses, even empires. They could also compete with their old bosses. Hope prospered in this new America.

The foundation of our Constitution came from the Bible. God writes: *"Let no debt remain outstanding, except the continuing debt to love one another, for he who loves his fellowman has fulfilled the law.*

The commandments, 'Do not commit adultery,' 'Do not murder,' 'Do not steal,' 'Do not covet,' and whatever other commandment there may be, are summed up in this one rule: 'Love your neighbor as yourself.' Love does no harm to its neighbor. Therefore love is the fulfillment of the law" (Romans 13:8-10).

In essence, if you love your neighbor, you fulfill all of God's laws. You love God by loving others.

> *"This is how we know what love is: Jesus Christ laid down his life for us. And we ought to lay down our lives for our brothers. If anyone has material possessions and sees his brother in need but has no pity on him, how can the love of God be in him? Dear children, let us not love with words or tongue but with actions and in truth."* (1 John 3:16-18)

If we don't show our love for others in a tangible way then, as the Scripture said, *"How can the love of God be in him?"*

The wisdom of God's greatest commandments serves as the foundation of our Constitution and Bill of Rights. This might explain how all the different people groups could come together and form such a great nation: "**OTHERS.**"

Our United States Constitution starts with a bang:

PREAMBLE TO THE CONSTITUTION

"We the People of the United States, **in Order to form a more perfect Union, establish Justice, insure domestic Tranquility, provide for the common defense, promote the general Welfare, and secure the Blessings of Liberty to ourselves and our Posterity,** do ordain and establish this Constitution for the United States of America."

The Preamble is one of the most important keys to understanding the Constitution.

Wikipedia states: "The Preamble to the United States Constitution is a brief <u>introductory statement</u> of the Constitution's fundamental purposes and guiding principles. It states in general terms, and courts have referred to it as reliable evidence of, the **Founding Fathers' intentions** regarding the Constitution's meaning and what they hoped the Constitution would achieve."

The Constitution established Congress (Senate and House of Representatives), the Executive Branch (President), and a Judicial Branch (Supreme Court and inferior courts). These three branches were to provide America a checks-and-balances system of Government.

All powers of our Government were divested in these three branches, their purpose was for the sake of the people **(OTHERS)**:

    A. A more perfect Union (of the people)

    B. Justice

    C. Peace

    D. Defense against other nations

    E. Promote general Welfare (of the people)

    F. Secure Blessings (from God) to the people and their families

The Founding Fathers recognized that the blessings from God came from God the Creator, and were given to men (Declaration of Independence). These blessings included certain rights that government couldn't take away (unalienable rights) such as *"life, liberty and the pursuit of happiness."* In enacting the Constitution, the Founding Fathers gave Government the responsibility to **secure these rights for the people** and for the benefit of the whole **United States of America (others).**

Notice it starts with *"We the people"* and ends with *"for the United States of America"* (**others**). In effect, **the Constitution is for the benefit of the nation**.

Sadly, Government has abandoned its original intent and the purpose given to it by the Founding Fathers and the Constitution. It has become a monster feeding off the people, using the guise of caring for the people as reason for its existence. Government has aligned itself with business interests and power groups and deviated from its original purpose. As it did, the people in the nation slowly changed focus from: "How can I help others?" to "How can I get mine!" A common theme in governmental hearings for new projects is, "Not in my back yard" (NIMBY). People's hearts have followed leadership's heart.

As the people saw elected leaders and its bureaucracy taking care of themselves first, they had to fight for their rights. They forget (or don't realize) that God said fools will only take care of themselves.

And as people had to fight for "theirs," they forgot the "unalienable rights" given to them by God. You don't have to fight for them, simply step into them. This is just like the early Christians who were persecuted, abused, taken advantage of, and even enslaved. Yet they walked with rights given them by their Creator; they walked in the Spirit, not in the flesh.

Did Jesus have a difficult time walking in His rights the day of His crucifixion?

Pick up your cross.

AMERICA'S GOVERNMENT IS NOT FOLLOWING THE PREAMBLE

The underlying reason for America's failure is that the people have elected "fools" to Government. According to God, these *"fools are corrupt, their deeds are vile."* They don't even do good for the very people who elected them. They find *"pleasure in evil conduct,"* and "*find no pleasure in understanding*" the responsibility given to them to create a more perfect union to bring justice and peace for the people.

They cannot comprehend that they were put in office by Creator God, because it was He who established the United States, and gave its Constitution: "*Everyone must submit himself to the governing authorities, for there is no authority except that which God has established. The authorities that exist have been established by God*" (Rom. 13:1).

God gave birth to America, established the authority structure of America and blessed our nation as our leaders followed the Constitution. It is obvious that America's current leadership — the Executive Branch, Legislative Branch and Judicial Branch — no longer follows the Constitution or its Preamble.

WHO'S AT FAULT?

Government is not to blame. It is foolish to blame fools. We, the people, are to blame. We stood by and watched while "fools" took over our government. We stood by as they placed other fools at the head of agencies, departments, and the bureaucracy. Granted, there are many in government who are not fools, and who have **others** in mind as they do their jobs. If this is you, don't get mad at me. I take my hat off to you for serving in government and trying to honor the Constitution.

And lest we fear standing by our foolish political leaders during the coming storm, let that thought perish. **God says we are responsible**:

> "...**If my people,** who are called by my name, will humble themselves and pray and seek my face and turn from their wicked ways, then will I hear from heaven and will forgive their sin and will heal their land." (2 Chronicles 7:14)

Our "*wicked ways,*" were that we stood by, doing nothing. We did not vote or passionately support God's cause in Government. **God Him-**

self, through our Founding Fathers, gave us the responsibility and authority to elect officials. They derive their "**just powers**" from us.

God is mad at us.

We cannot blame Government for the state it is in today. We should submit ourselves to these authorities and pray for them.

God has judgment set aside for the fools who reject him, but He also has strong discipline for His children who neglect His Word and their duty. What if all the ramifications of God "*frustrating*" the "fools" accrues upon His Namesake, the Christians?

If God is bringing discipline on America, the poor will be severely impacted. What if God blames Christians for the trouble upon the poor due to our neglect to elect the righteous?

The Lord told Moses to appoint men with certain qualities:

> "*But select capable men from all the people — men who fear God, trustworthy men who hate dishonest gain — and appoint them as officials over thousands, hundreds, fifties and tens. Have them serve as judges for the people at all times….*" (Exodus 18:21-22)

GOD'S QUESTION:	GOD'S ANSWER:
Have we elected capable men?	No, we have elected many "fools."
Have we elected men who fear God?	No, we have appointed "fools."
Have we elected trustworthy men?	No, fools are not trustworthy.
Have we elected men who hate dishonest gain?	No, fools love gain at any cost.

REALITIES TODAY: THERE'S GLASS IN MY PUDDING
A MORE PERFECT UNION

The Preamble gives us the purpose of the Constitution: **"in Order to form a more perfect Union...."** Does a more perfect Union exist today? If America stayed true to its course, our nation would have gotten better and better. It did until after World War II. **Has it improved since?** (If so, why do political parties stubbornly fight in Congress while the people are hurting?)

To answer, let's look at some of the reaming realities and stunning statistics of our America.

PEOPLE NOT IN LABOR FORCE

The number of people in poverty has grown exponentially in the last 20 years. The best measure for employment and job improvement in America is "People not in Labor Force." This statistic includes people not working, but also those on disabilities, as well as those who have ceased looking for work. (Many have been out-of-work for over a year. They've given up.) The government claims that things have improved based on unemployment being reduced. However, have things really gotten better when people have given up looking for work? Presently there are over 100 million people not in the work force. (figure 3, page 93)

God is frustrating America. (1 Cor. 1:19)

FOOD STAMPS (INDICATOR OF WELFARE)

People on Welfare and Food Stamps (SNAP) have also increased dramatically. See the comprehensive eight-year chart for Food Stamp usage. In 2006, America had approximately 28 million on Food Stamps. By 2013 that number grew to 47 million. (figure 4, page 93)

God is frustrating America. (1 Cor. 1:19)

NUCLEAR FAMILY

We do not have a "more perfect union" because America has not taken care of her nuclear family. It is defined as "a family group consisting of a pair of adults and their biological children" (Wikipedia). This term is being redefined by liberals to include different parent groups, such as stepparents, and any mix of children including stepchildren. See the chart that reflects the shift in nuclear family over the past 40 years. The nuclear family comprised roughly 40% of families in 1970. By 2000, that number dropped to roughly 24%. I suspect that number is now below 20%. (figure 5, page 94)

God is frustrating America. (1 Cor. 1:19)

CHILDREN BORN TO UNWED MOTHERS

In the past 60 years, the number of children born to unwed mothers has grown from under 5% to over 40% (2010). This has severely damaged the American nuclear family and families in general. As our Preamble states, we have not "secure(d) the Blessings of Liberty to ourselves and our Posterity." (www.FamilyFacts.org) (figure 6, page 94)

God is frustrating America. (1 Cor. 1:19)

ABORTION

America has had 56 million abortions since 1973. (Christian Life Resources, US Abortion Statistics By Year 1973-Current)

God is frustrating America. (1 Cor. 1:19)

JUSTICE

Justice is waning as our courts are jammed. The rich too often skirt justice while the poor do not know what justice looks like. It's almost as if someone has rewritten the laws of the land so that the Constitution is unrecognizable.

Edwin Meese III once wrote:

"...Overcriminalization represents a serious threat to both individual liberty and public safety.... It leads to the point where criminal law and criminal punishment become nothing more than convenient and effective tools of government power....

"The path of overcriminalization represents for some of our policymakers a misapprehension of the essential nature and purpose of the criminal law. For others, it reflects, sadly, a deliberate effort to remake society using criminal law as the agent of sociological change...But using the criminal process in a politicized manner to change society violates our nation's concepts of individual liberty, limited government, and consent of the governed. It is the method of a tyrannical state, not a democratic republic...." (One Nation Under Arrest, Authors Paul Rosenzwieg, Brian W. Walsh, Intro xii-xiii, Heritage Foundation, Washington, D.C.)

MORE LAWS, MORE JUSTICE?

"...The most complete count of federal crimes, done by the U.S. Department of Justice (DOJ) in the early 1980s, put the number at 3,000. A 1998 report by a task force of the American Bar Association relied on the DOJ figure and other data to measure the growth of federal criminal law but did not itself actually provide a count of federal crimes. In a 2004 Federalist Society monograph building on the DOJ and ABA reports, I counted new federal crimes enacted following the point at which the ABA report finished its data collection at the close of 1996. That report estimates that there were 4,000 federal crimes at the start of 2000. This report updates that total through 2007, finding 452 additional crimes created since 2007, for a total of at least 4,450 federal crimes." (Heritage Foundation, Legal Memorandum #26, June 16, 2008-Revisiting the Explosive Growth of Federal Crimes, By John S. Baker)

God is frustrating America. (1 Cor. 1:19)

PEACE

Peace within our society is disappearing. This disappearance has accelerated in the last 20-30 years. Anxiety and depression is at epidemic levels, especially in the workplace.

STATISTICS: Americans Affected by Mental Illness

· One in four adults–approximately 61.5 million Americans–experiences mental illness in a given year.

· One in 17–about 13.6 million–live with a serious mental illness such as schizophrenia, major depression or bipolar disorder.

· Approximately (~) 20% of youth ages 13-18 experience severe mental disorders in a given year. For ages 8-15, the estimate is 13%.

· ~1.1% American adults (2.4 million) live with schizophrenia.

· ~2.6% American adults (6.1 million) live with bipolar disorder.

· ~ 6.7% American adults (14.8 million) live with major depression.

· ~18.1% American adults (42 million) live with anxiety disorders, such as panic disorder, obsessive-compulsive disorder (OCD), post-traumatic stress disorder (PTSD), generalized anxiety disorder and phobias.

· ~9.2 million adults have co-occurring mental health and addiction disorders.

· ~26% homeless adults staying in shelters live with serious mental illness. An estimated 46% live with severe mental illness and/or substance use disorders.

(http://www.nami.org/factsheets/mentalillness_factsheet.pdf)

People are on all kinds of drugs and medication.

Deaths due to medication and drug use are at an all-time high.

Illegal drug use is out of control — marijuana, cocaine, heroine, ice and many others.

God is frustrating America. (1 Cor. 1:19)

DEFENSE AGAINST OTHER NATIONS

Government has also misapplied the concept to "provide for the common defense." The world thinks it needs to defend against Uncle Sam. As a result, resources are being misallocated: people, talent, and money. A crazy old quote says, "If you don't know where you are going any road can take you there." (SOURCE: Lewis Carroll, "Alice in Wonderland.") Our government has taken all the wrong roads and are now dumbfounded at the number of dead ends they've hit.

God is frustrating America. (1 Cor. 1:19)

PROMOTE GENERAL WELFARE (OF THE PEOPLE)

The "fools" in office have figured out an excellent plan to keep themselves in office and made sure they'll be very well compensated. The average government worker (most are unionized) are better off than the average private worker. They also take care of businesses, and the businesses help them get reelected. It's a cozy relationship. (Not all in government have this ulterior motivation.)

Politicians give out money and benefits to the poor and those poor who care enough to vote reelect them; it's hard not to. They have strayed from promoting the general welfare of society, to taking custodial responsibility of possibly 50 million Americans, as well as providing sustenance living for an additional 50 million more. This enables millions and disables many more families.

God is frustrating America. (1 Cor. 1:19)

SECURE THE BLESSINGS (FROM GOD) TO THE PEOPLE (PROSPERITY)

These blessings included certain rights that government couldn't take away, "unalienable rights" including "life, liberty and the pursuit of happiness." But they also included the ability for upward mobility in all areas of American life and lifestyles. If the average man were to rate — on scale of 1-10, 10 being best — these blessings in the 1900-1950 period, I believe Americans might give a composite grade of 8.5.

Today, Americans might give a grade of 3.0. (My book, so I give the grades.)

God is frustrating America. (1 Cor. 1:19)

WHAT HAPPENED TO THE BLESSINGS?

The grasp and girth of government is growing like a Goliath monster, gobbling everything in its path. Government is too large. America will soon learn that throwing money at well-intended programs without a strong foundation in our source, God, leads to greed in the very people we're trying to help.

As of 2015, the United States debt is $18 Trillion.

U.S. unfunded liabilities are over $100 Trillion (Forbes, "You Think the Deficit Is Bad? Federal Unfunded Liabilities Exceed $127 Trillion," 1/17/2014, Vance Ginn.) These are for our Social Security and Medicare programs.

The US deficit is close to $1 Trillion a year.
All taxes collected approximate $3 Trillion.
All Expenditures approximate $3.8 Trillion.
Number of working people is shrinking.
Number of people not working is growing.

"The 102.159 million Americans not working in December is not the all-time record of Americans not working. That all-time record was set in October 2013, at 102.896 million. The employment-population ratio that month was an even more pitiful 58.2%." (Forbes, 1/24/2014, Peter Ferrara)

Average wage of middle class families in the last 10-15 years has lost ground (inflation adjusted).

Mass shootings are out of control.
Sexual attacks on college campuses are rampant.
Christians have lost their religious freedom.

OUR CHILDREN WILL NOT BE BLESSED

"A new Wall Street Journal/NBC News poll found that despite the steady pace of hiring in recent months, 76% of adults lack confidence that their children's generation will have a better life than they do—an all-time high. Some 71% of adults think the country is on the wrong track, a leap of 8 points from a June survey, and 60% believe the U.S. is in a state of decline." (Wall Street Journal, "Poll Finds Widespread Economic Anxiety," Patrick O'Connor, updated Aug. 5, 2014)

AMERICA'S MAJOR POLICY DISASTERS

MIDEAST

America fought her most recent wars defending freedom in Iraq and Afghanistan, but is now losing all gains paid for by the blood of America's soldiers. The Executive branch claimed victory over Al Qaida and Taliban terrorists while, at this writing (Fall 2014) ISIS is taking over Iraq and creating an Islamic State (or caliphate) in the mid-East.

VETERANS CARE

America cannot care for her Veterans, especially those who fought in the past 10 years. Media outlets report that 57,000 Veterans have waited more than 90 days for an appointment. An additional 64,000 never made it to waiting lists and may have fallen through the cracks.

V.A.'s own audit found that 13% of V.A. schedulers were told to falsify appointment request dates to make patient wait times appear shorter. Further, at least one instance of that fraud was found at 76% V.A. facilities.

"This report makes it clear that the only people benefiting from our current V.A. healthcare system are the bureaucrats who put their own bonuses over veterans' care," said Sen. John Cornyn (R-Tex.). (Washington Post, 6/9/14)

ASIA

Russia is presently on the move; while, simultaneously, what American President Obama says counts for ZERO. This is a complete reversal from the past when what America said counted. Presidents John F. Kennedy, Ronald Reagan, George H.W. Bush, and George W. Bush had positive influence on the world scene. When they spoke, the world paid attention.

AMERICA'S BORDER WITH MEXICO

It is surreal that America could have the kind of border crisis that it is currently having, with tens of thousands of children without parents or adult supervision simply walking across the border and thinking they will be welcomed in the United States. Congress passed HR 7311 known as the "William Wilberforce Trafficking Victims Protection Reauthorization Act of 2008." Some Amendments help us understand the law:

Section 107(a) of Trafficking Victims Protection Act of 2000 (22 U.S.C. 7105(a)) is amended:

" '(F) '(i) increased protections for refugees and internally displaced persons, including outreach and education efforts to prevent such refugees and internally displaced persons from being exploited by traffickers; and

'(ii) performance of best interest determinations for **unaccompanied and separated children** who come to the attention of the United Nations High Commissioner for Refugees, its partner organizations, or any organization that contracts with the Department of State in order to identify child trafficking victims and to assist their safe integration, reintegration, and resettlement.'"

The bill continues:

"'SEC. 107A. INCREASING EFFECTIVENESS OF ANTI-TRAFFICKING PROGRAMS.
'(2) REQUIREMENTS- In carrying out paragraph (1), the President shall--
'(c) Evaluation of Anti-Trafficking Programs-
'(1) IN GENERAL—The **President** shall establish a system to evaluate the effectiveness and efficiency of the assistance provided under anti-trafficking programs established under this Act on a program-by-program basis in order to **maximize the long-term sustainable development impact of such assistance**.

'(A) establish **performance goals** for the assistance described in paragraph (1), expressed in an objective and quantifiable form, to the extent practicable;
'(B) ensure that **performance indicators** are used for programs

authorized under this Act to measure and assess the achievement of the performance goals described in subparagraph (A);

'(C) provide a **basis for recommendations for adjustments to the assistance** described in paragraph (1) to enhance the impact of such assistance; and

'(D) ensure that **evaluations are conducted** by subject matter experts in and outside the United States Government, to the extent practicable."

The President was given the responsibility to set up performance goals and monitor the program. President Obama's failure to respond stems from his seeming inability to comprehend the underlying intent and seriousness of the problem — like a deer paralyzed in oncoming headlights. God is "frustrating" his ability to lead the nation. The solution is actually simple; the President just has to ask. If Obama would ask God, God would guide him. If he thinks he knows what to do, then he can use his pen and his telephone. However, wisdom from God is beyond Obama's reach.

MORE HORROR AHEAD

1. People in government who do not fear God and go after dishonest gain use the Internal Revenue Service (I.R.S.) to do their dirty work. The I.R.S. has been used by the Powers-in-Control to attack conservative groups, Tea Party groups, and conservative businesses. The same I.R.S. will manage ObamaCare. This will not turn out well, in fact much worse than the Veteran Healthcare tragedy.

2. The Veterans' Health debacle is an advance warning of how bureaucracy does not work. The focus of the bureaucracy is gain for themselves.

3. The more government tries to fix things, the worse it will get. Government bureaucracy is missing something: **wisdom from God**. Naturally, this does not apply to Christians in government.

SUPERRICH: THE RICH TAKE & TAKE & TAKE

The superrich — also called the upper "1%" — are slowly squeezing out small and mid-size businesses. They may also have stolen opportunity from the middle class. They rule their business worlds with profit as the sole consideration. *"Ruthless men gain only wealth,"* (Proverbs 11:16 b).

The 1% work with Congress (through Super Pacs), spend millions of dollars to help "their" candidates get elected. When they have needs, such as laws that help them benefit, one phone call through an agent and deals are sealed.

Why do people not trust government? People in government need to get elected and the rich provide the funds. It takes a man of strong character to stand for others ahead of themselves. God gave Moses his criteria. America might do well to follow God's selection process: *"But select capable men from all the people — men who fear God, trustworthy men who hate dishonest gain…"* (Exodus 18:21).

People who rise up in politics gain power and influence. All who run for office are capable, but unless they fear God and are *"trustworthy men who hate dishonest gain,"* they will inevitably succumb to temptation. They'll end up seeking for themselves instead of for the people.

America was built on God's principle of helping "others." This is a truth in the Declaration of Independence and the Preamble of the Constitution. It's the very foundation of Jesus' heart:

> *"You see, at just the right time, when we were still powerless, Christ died for the ungodly. Very rarely will anyone die for a righteous man, though for a good man someone might possibly dare to die. But God demonstrates his own love for us in this: While we were still sinners, Christ died for us."* (Rom. 5:6-8)

William Booth, founder of the Salvation Army sent out a telegram in the early 1900s to the Salvation Army leaders. Not one to waste money or words, the telegram had one word: "Others." America has lost this foundational Christian ideal.

1. Politics is busted: Controlled by the rich because they get what they want.
2. Government. Government is controlled by the rich.
3. Wall Street- Financial- Wealth. Wall Street is concerned with more and more for itself.
4. Economically- Can our kids make a living?
5. Law rules, attorneys rule. Much of the bureaucracy ends up doing things so they don't get sued. They are not making decisions for the sake of the "others." Legal system end up with judges being appointed who have liberal values, not the values of God, or "We the people."

WHAT ARE THEY AFTER?

One of the most illogical-yet-common fallacies is how people chase after happiness. However, God has a truth: people can only be happy if they are happy in others. The Bible says this:

"And why do you worry about clothes? See how the lilies of the field grow. They do not labor or spin. Yet I tell you that not even Solomon in all his splendor was dressed like one of these. If that is how God clothes the grass of the field, which is here today and tomorrow is thrown into the fire, will he not much more clothe you, O you of little faith? So do not worry, saying, 'What shall we eat?' or 'What shall we drink?' or 'What shall we wear?' For the pagans run after all these things, and your heavenly Father knows that you need them. But seek first his kingdom and his righteousness, and all these things will be given to you as well. Therefore do not worry about tomorrow, for tomorrow will worry about itself. Each day has enough trouble of its own." (Matthew 6:28-34)

Jesus teaches us: People, do not worry that your clothes make you look better than the next person — more hip, suave, sexy, classy. Be content with the way God clothes and provides for you. Be content with what God provides for you to eat and drink. Recognize that God provides.

Our challenge is to *"seek first his kingdom and his righteousness,"* and God will provide these things as well. People seeking and chasing after these things, thinking they'll provide happiness, only end up empty. It's the surest way to destroy the body, soul and spirit. Easy to preach, not easy to live.

MISGUIDED GOALS

Why do we have tens of millions of people in depression and many more in anxiety when we live in the richest nation in the world? Why is Congress forced to pass thousands of laws to keep people in check? Why must Government enforce a level-and-fair playing field so everyone can have an equal shot at happiness? The system is broken.

Over the past 50 years, we've ended up in an America that has changed our Constitution and the very focus established in the Bill of Rights. The bottom line: **America has forgotten God**.

God gave us unalienable rights. Yet our citizens are left to fight for their "rights." Further, Government is destroying the rights of many groups. America is going down the tubes. Instead of a unified America that stands strong, we are a house divided, fighting one another. We will fall.

THE POOR: LEFT OUT IN THE COLD

The result of our disobedience (mine included) has disproportionately affected the poor in America. The sun and rain fall evenly on all America, but the different groups of poor do not have resources like umbrellas, cars, homes or savings to help them through such storms.

GOD HAS A PLAN: HE'S DOING SOMETHING WITH AMERICA

"And we know that God causes everything to work together for the good of those who love God and are called according to his purpose for them." (Rom 8:28-29, NLT)

God has a plan and He will move in the world and in America to execute His plan.

WHAT IS GOD DOING?

What if God is allowing the breakdown of America to test the hearts of Christians who profess to love Jesus?

What if God is not causing the turmoil and trouble within our America, but instead is allowing *"fools"* to take over to test what we would do?

What if God is using all that is taking place to work out the maximum good in the maximum number of people, each growing the maximum amount in the shortest timeframe?

What if God is not doing anything except testing the faith of those who profess to trust Him?

We may not know God's intent; however, in the same way that there is level ground at the foot of the cross, **now that America is busted, all Christians have an equal opportunity to please God.**

Where will those impacted by the broken government and bureaucracy turn? To a broken government to solve the problem? The same broken government that helped to create the problems?

Can we make a difference in the lives of those severely disadvantaged by the policies of government?

Living out our Christian faith, especially when we think we know the problem, is easier said than done. However, here are some relevant Christian beliefs:

God is in control and we must trust Him.

When you lose your job because someone scammed the bosses, **we must trust Him.**

When we lose our business due to bankruptcy, **we must trust Him.**

When the banks "call our loan" and create havoc in our businesses, **we must trust Him.**

When our customers fail to pay us and create a severe cash flow problem, **we must trust Him.**

When our kids get into drugs, alcoholism, sex, evil and wickedness, **we must trust Him.**

When our kids scam us because of their situation and condition, **we must trust Him.**

When someone goes on a shooting rampage and our grandkids get shot, **we must trust Him.**

When a terrorist hijacks a plane, or bombs a vacation resort where our family is staying, severely injuring them or worse, **we must trust Him.**

When politicians lie to us (i.e. "You can keep your healthcare plan and your doctors too"), **we must trust Him.**

When government favors an adversary and they get a contract, **we must trust Him.**

When Social Services breakdown and medical attention that our loved ones require fall short, hurting your favorite family member, **we must trust Him.** (Example: V.A. cannot take care of its own veterans, then "cook the books" to cover up over 50,000 veterans waiting over 90 days for needed medical care. Can you imagine how bad it will be with ObamaCare?)

When Government passes laws contrary to our Constitution and with impunity, **we must trust Him.** (Example: Prohibiting the use of public schools to conservative groups because they "violate" the rights of L.G.B.T.)

When Government takes away freedoms guaranteed by the Constitution, using bureaucracy to do its dirty work (i.e. having the I.R.S. target conservative groups), **we must trust Him.**

Are these situations (and thousands more) the result of sinful and evil men?

Could God be orchestrating and intentionally allowing wickedness so America goes through suffering and pain, and ultimately get stronger with God?

Is this the same as God hardening Pharaoh's heart?

Could God be looking to Christians to do something?

Could a good God bring suffering on His people for a purpose? What might that purpose be?

GOD'S THOUGHTS

"Who is going to harm you if you are eager to do good? But even if you should suffer for what is right, you are blessed. 'Do not fear what they fear; do not be frightened.' But in your hearts set apart Christ as Lord. Always be prepared to give an answer to everyone who asks you to give the reason for the hope that you have. But do this with gentleness and respect, keeping a clear conscience, so that those who speak maliciously against your good behavior in Christ may be ashamed of their slander. It is better, if it is God's will, to suffer for doing good than for doing evil. For Christ died for sins once for all, the righteous for the unrighteous, to bring you to God. He was put to death in the body but made alive by the Spirit...." (1 Peter 3:13-18)

"If you suffer, it should not be as a murderer or thief or any other kind of criminal, or even as a meddler. However, if you suffer as a Christian, do not be ashamed, but praise God that you bear that name. For it is time for judgment to begin with the family of God; and if it begins with us, what will the outcome be for those who do not obey the gospel of God? And, 'If it is hard for the righteous to be saved, what will become of the ungodly and the sinner?' So then, those who suffer according to God's will should commit themselves to their faithful Creator and continue to do good." (1 Peter 4:15-19)

"Remember this, fix it in mind, take it to heart, you rebels. Remember the former things, those of long ago; **I am God, and there is no other; I am God, and there is none like me***. I make known the end from the beginning, from ancient times, what is still to come. I say: My purpose will stand, and I will do all that I please. From the east I summon a bird of prey; from a far-off land, a man to fulfill my purpose.* **What I have said, that will I bring about; what I have planned, that will I do***. Listen to me, you stubborn-hearted, you who are far from righteousness. I am bringing my righteousness near, it is not far away; and my salvation will not be delayed. I will grant salvation to Zion, my splendor to Israel."* (Isaiah 46:8-13)

In Isaiah, God brought discipline on Israel for rebelling against Him, disobeying His commands and desires. He uses a nation from the east (Medo-Persians via King Cyrus) to discipline Israel so that His salvation would come to Israel.

God uses Hosea to tell Israel something similar: *"For I will be like a lion to Ephraim, like a great lion to Judah. I will tear them to pieces and go away; I will carry them off, with no one to rescue them.* **Then I will go back to my place until they admit their guilt. And they will seek my face; in their misery they will earnestly seek me"** (Hosea 5:14-15).

God is bringing America (and the world) to the destruction of our way of life as discipline. We must fall on our faces, turn from our wicked ways, call out to Him, and then He may heal the land:

> *"When I shut up the heavens so that there is no rain, or command locusts to devour the land or send a plague among my people, **if my people, who are called by my name,** will humble themselves and pray and seek my face and turn from their wicked ways, then will I hear from heaven and will forgive their sin and will heal their land."* (2 Chronicles 7:13-14)

America is busted, yet God is working for the good of Christians and for the good of America. Does He want to use you in this endeavor? Is God waiting for you to respond? Ready?

If He called you, would you hear His voice?

CHAPTER 3

AMERICA THE BANKRUPT

"He who increases his wealth by exorbitant interest
amasses it for another, who will be kind to the poor."
(Proverbs 28:8)

"To the man who pleases him,
God gives wisdom, knowledge and happiness,
but to the sinner he gives the task of gathering and storing
up wealth to hand it over to the one who pleases God.
This too is meaningless, a chasing after the wind."
(Ecclesiastes 2:26)

BEAUTY WITHOUT FINANCIAL STRENGTH?

As we enter into a vibrant relationship with Jesus, we realize He is all we need for life and godliness. Jesus says that if we love Him, we'll obey Him and then life works. Why? Because the things He tells us are good for every aspect of our lives: love for God, family, in-laws; how to manage work relationships, finances, jobs, money, sex ... our whole lives.

All of these major facets of life are intertwined. Life does not work well if one part is out of sync. When that happens, **God uses an out-of-sync life to get us in sync with Him**.

Our focus will be **money: How we view it and how we handle it has a vital impact on our Christian walk**. Specifically, when a "point of tension" hits our pocketbooks — whether business or family finances — it can feel like we're walking with rocks in our shoes. We need to be prepared.

Let's take a 50,000-feet elevation view of the financial condition of our world and our country. We do this to understand how it has already impacted us and how it will continue to do so. We will also "connect the dots" to see if God is involved. As we look at the data and my analysis, keep in mind that I'm **not predicting a dooms-day scenario**. Christians will thrive through even the worst situation: **God will work for our good, and we will grow and flow through it**.

However, I see a rocky road ahead: A severe depression will hit the world and America. It's possible it has already hit you. Many are experiencing the first wave of its impact: If your neighbor and community are out of work, or have lost homes, you clearly see the recession. Then again, when you lose your job or business and your family is directly affected, you know the depression personally.

As America is headed into an economic and financial storm, all Americans will be severely affected. However, **proper handling and attitude toward money as God teaches will help us maneuver through the economic disaster ahead**. More importantly, I believe God is involved in what is happening financially in America. That blessed assurance means that if we believe He is orchestrating good, we can adapt to even the worst situations.

GOD CONNECTS INTERESTS

Most of my life was spent learning: being educated in business, then on-the-job learning through running the family business and managing our business assets. Any successful businessperson has to be confident and knowledgeable. I was no different. Once I established a relationship with Jesus, I recognized that it was by God's Hand that any good came to our business: *WOW, it wasn't really me!*

Still, I gained a little knowledge in many areas. God took that knowledge and blessed me with a little wisdom: *"God gave Solomon wisdom and very great insight, and a breadth of understanding as measureless as the sand on the seashore"* (1 Kings 4:29-30).

I'll admit that if Solomon had a wisdom rating of 100, I'm not even at a 10. My wife will attest to that. I have no idea how God gives wisdom, but I surmise He must begin with basic knowledge. In other words, He doesn't give wisdom to a dummy.

ROOSEVELT HIGH & UNIVERSITY OF HAWAII

Upon graduating from high school, I headed straight into a college degree in Electrical Engineering. The one thing I did not want to do was become an electrician. My mom and dad never tried to steer me, but now I can see that God was involved. He knew I needed an education as a base for knowledge training. He guided my steps even before I knew Him.

I used to think that I never used my electrical engineering education. I thought I'd forgotten 90% of my equations 10 years after I graduated. I don't remember any calculus, physics, thermodynamics, or Boolean algebra. And programming consisted of Fortran, which was typed into paper cards with rectangular holes. A bit outdated!

Over the past 40 years, I've come to realize that my degree was not so much about learning equations and solving problems. It was God developing in me a basis for learning and resolving life.

DESIRE & "BETTER LEARN THIS"

Once I joined Dad's business, I discovered a desire to learn everything. I had a desire to do greater things so I thought I'd better learn it all. I started reading many topics: finances, economics, business principles, management, accounting, self-improvement (Og Mandino, "The Greatest Salesman").

A little learning can be dangerous to your health. How can one really know if he knows enough? How can one really know if he's learned the right thing? If he's applying principles correctly?

As I was learning in the 70s, I went all in and bet the company—everything my dad had worked for over 20 years. The reason I could do so confidently is because I had knowledge. I analyzed costs and developed more sophisticated installation rates all because I had developed a state-of-the-art cost accounting system. I overlooked one small thing.

What our crew of electricians could do on a small project would not necessarily apply on a large project. Big difference! The big general contractors had different construction methods: flying forms, slip forms, jump forms; they wouldn't allow us to penetrate their construction forms and the complexities in our installation "killed us." We hadn't learned how to deal with these issues. Our electricians had a difficult time trying to service customers with whom they had no relationship. Relationships take time. Instead, we developed a "mainland style," dog-eat-dog business practice.

The main problem was I thought I knew; I didn't yet know what Paul had written: "…*We know that we all possess knowledge. Knowledge puffs up, but love builds up. The man who thinks he knows something does not yet know as he ought to know…*" (1 Cor. 8:1-2).

God's plan was in motion at that time, humbling me. I wasn't completely humbled, but at least He cut me down by 50%. (Sorry, I'm a numbers guy.) Lots to go then and lots to go still. I continued learning and returned to Peter Drucker's work on management. Drucker is a Christian and his business principles are from God. My goal was to have each of our employees live His principles. It became the foundation of God's work in A-1 A-Lectrician.

BUSINESS & SIGNS OF THE TIMES

The Bible deals with business principles and signs of the times. The key to understanding these times is to understand God's global view. He provides insight to how He works, what He desires, and what He plans to do. And He gives access to anyone who desires it, freely available in His Word.

Yet this is only a basic understanding; God whets our appetite for deeper wisdom. At His discretion, God can give more wisdom by grace. If we follow His basic principles, we may be given greater godly wisdom from Him.

For example, a simple principle: *"The rich rule over the poor, and the borrower is servant to the lender"* (Prov. 22:7) could have saved a lot of grief during the 2008-09 downturn, especially in housing.

I AM NOT AN EXPERT, SO WHAT ARE THE QUESTIONS?

This is not a financial or economic book and I certainly am no expert. Simply, it is an analysis from God's perspective of what is taking place today as it lines up with Bible prophecy. We will also take into account management, business, financial, economic, as well as geo-political concepts. Finally we'll consider **"What"** might happen, as well as **How** and **When** it may happen.

It's like buying stock: You may be right about which stock to buy yet go broke because you are wrong on timing. God's Word teaches the importance of timing: *"Therefore Jesus told them, 'The **right time** for me has not yet come; for you any time is right'"* (Jn. 7:6).

<u>The best place to start to "understand the times" is by asking the right questions:</u>

A. Who are the powers in control of the world today?

B. Who controls government?

C. Who controls the world's economies?

D. What is the interrelationship of all of the above factors?

E. Can we hope to understand the impact of a social, economic and/ or financial collapse?

F. Will we know if a collapse takes place? How will we recognize if any type of collapse is underway?

G. Does it matter?

H. What part does the Bible play in these considerations?

I. Could God have a plan in this area?

J. Is there a connection between any of this and the poor?

K. How will events impact each of the five areas of poor? And, more importantly, how might that affect me? Finally, what is God telling us?

BEAUTY OF AMERICA CONNECTED TO GOD

For two hundred years, America was beautiful. America was blessed thanks to foundational principles given by our Founding Fathers, who recognized the Bible: *"Lord, you establish peace for us; all that we have accomplished you have done for us"* (Isa. 26:12). Only God can bring peace on the land. Only God can bring healing to the land.

It starts with recognizing that all lasting accomplishment comes from God. Alexis de Toqueville said: "Not until I went into the **churches of America** and heard her pulpits aflame with righteousness did I understand the secret of her genius and power. America is great because she is good, and if America ever ceases to be good, she will cease to be great."

God made America great through people who love God. Those who didn't have a relationship with Him still benefitted. There is intrinsic beauty in America as she believes and lives out the principles in the Declaration of Independence. This beauty comes from God. It was our Constitution that enabled America's beauty to thrive for almost 200 years.

TWO KEYS IN THE DECLARATION

First, America's new focus on rights flips our Declaration and Constitution upside down. Rights focus on laws. Therefore, our government is constantly rewriting laws of the land to protect the rights of whoever is in power. This was never the intent of our Founding Fathers. Their focus was on God and the people's relationship with Him was central to the Constitution.

The Founding Fathers and early America knew this and her whole Constitution consisted of only a few pages. America did right because she recognized her Creator's power and divine nature, so she lived *"without excuses."* She knew there was a coming Day of Judgment.

The second key principle in the Declaration is that **God gave Americans a responsibility to maintain** *"unalienable rights."* The Founding Fathers recognized that God orchestrated the founding of America, its Constitution, and its government. Therefore, government derives its authority from God: *"Everyone must submit himself to the governing authorities, for there is no authority except that which God has established. The authorities that exist have been established by God"* (Rom. 13:1).

This is not happening today. We've disobeyed and disregarded God's structure in our government. Since we've abandoned God's commands in America, God has withdrawn His hedge of protection around our country.

Recently, I participated in a prayer walk at the State Capitol. We had just a small group but as this is written, we are a week before the primary elections of 2014. We wanted to park in underground parking at the State Capitol but were surprised when police had it closed off.

So we parked across the street and walked over. One of our members asked the news cameraman what was going on. Someone had left a backpack on the grounds of the Department of Health. We spent 30 minutes praying over the Capitol, for the election, for honest men and women to rise up, for the voters to rise up, and so forth.

As we walked back, the police had closed off Beretania Street headed Ewa (west). It was a traffic jam. The news later reported that it was just a harmless backpack. That one forgotten backpack resulted in 10 policemen, multiple news crews, thousands of cars diverted, and many people "pissed off."

We the people are losing our freedom.

AMERICA THE UGLY

Some argue that America is still a great place to live. I agree. But not as beautiful as it was. Nor is it as beautiful as God had intended it to be. Many Americans are not experiencing life, liberty and happiness.

We have freedom to travel and fly anywhere we want, but not all can afford it. When people do travel, there is fear of terrorists; people are upset at security and the lines; people are anxious.

People are worried about shootings in the work place, shopping malls, on the streets, on military bases, in our grade schools, middle schools, high schools and colleges. People are anxious.

People working are concerned about losing their jobs. People who are not working are concerned about finding a job and paying bills. Then there are millions who are not working and haven't for over a year; they've lost motivation. Add to that the millions who can work but are collecting Social Security Disability and are worried that they will lose benefits. People are anxious.

People who are working are worried about retirement. Can they retire at 62 or 65? How long will funds last? How will they pay for medical coverage? People are anxious.

People are taking more pills than ever: uppers and downers. Pills to get going; pills to wind down; pills to sleep; pills to stay up. People are anxious.

People are turning to alcohol, prescription drugs, illegal drugs, ice, cocaine, marijuana, heroin; they are shooting, snorting, free-basing and smoking; they're even using legal substances to get high, but I'll not go there! People are anxious.

The sad "sleight of hand" focus on rights (rather than on Creator God) has led America to her lowest level in history. "Women's rights" lead to 50 million babies aborted. People's "right to get stoned" lead to the legalization of marijuana in several states... and more coming. People's "right to be entertained and to gamble" is leading to a casino in every state. The "right" to sue for damages is now out of control. And "gay rights" has taken over many states and lead to millions marrying the same sex. Soon "transvestite rights" will lead to unisex restrooms. People are anxious.

Yet everyone has rights. The "right" to not work and yet demand government take care of them. The "right" to medical coverage "free of charge" yet paid for by the working class. The "right" to a free education, yet it will not be used for productive purposes. The "right" of an artist to express oneself, regardless of who they offend. People are anxious.

AMERICA: LIVING ON BORROWED TIME

America is living on borrowed time, time borrowed from our children. We've spent trillions of dollars from the future income of our children, money never to be repaid. The foundation of any good family is to provide a better future for their children, which brings hope.

Our children today are the first generation that can look forward to a lower standard of living. We've gone astray from the original mission of our Founding Fathers.

My father left me a business to run. In very simple terms, the business had a positive net worth when he put me in charge and was taken up by God. If he had left me a business with a negative net worth and no way to dig our way out, I wouldn't be writing this book today.

America has done exactly that to our children: We've left them a tremendous debt and not a very pretty future. One may argue it cannot be assigned to each citizen, except that government will charge them greater taxes. We are leaving a national debt of over $18 trillion. (figure 7, page 95)

And growing.

Chart C3E2 shows the increase of the U.S. National Debt over the past 50 years. Based on current projections and future unfunded liabilities the debt will never be paid off. Greater horror could arise if the dollar is not the world currency, especially as interest rates rise. An article in "Forbes" helps us understand: "Unfunded liabilities is the difference between the net present value of expected future government spending and the net present value of projected future tax revenue, particularly those associated with Social Security and Medicare." It puts the number at **$127 trillion**. (Vance Ginn, "You Think The Deficit Is Bad? Federal Unfunded Liabilities Exceed $127 Trillion," 1/17/2014.) (figure 8, page 96)

PREAMBLE IS DEAD

The Founding Fathers were concerned with creating "**a more perfect Union...domestic Tranquility,**" translated: peace and times of refreshing, a Biblical model. Also, "promoting the general Welfare," another Biblical model: taking care of others. Also, to "**secure**

the Blessings of Liberty to ourselves and our Posterity," yet another Biblical model of blessing our children with a better life.

Sadly, America is moving in the wrong direction on all three counts.

There were almost 47 million people living in poverty in 2012, of which there were 16 million children. There is no common measure for middle class Americans. So I will take the liberty of using U.S. Census Data: 2011 Household Income Table of Contents, Chart for All Races. Using an arbitrary income range of $40,000 to $84,999 and adding the number of people in that range, we'll call that the "middle class." There are approximately 51 million people in this range as of 2011. By all indications (see charts in Chapter 6) this group is losing purchasing power as well as abilities for home ownership and college educations for their children. www.census.gov/hhes/www/cpstables/032012/hhinc/hinc03_000.htm

The American "middle class" is living with a declining standard of living. This means their children will find it more difficult to buy homes and establish roots in one central community. The Bureau of Labor Statistics did a study in which the average American changed jobs every 3-4 years or so (BLS News Release 7/25/12, www.bls.gov/news.release/pdf/nlsoy.pdf). "He" works and lives among strangers, separated from family. He travels once or twice a year to visit family. God created the family to bring peace and stability to people by connecting them together, even over multiple generations.

Could God be bringing the family back together? (We'll explore this more in Chapter 6.)

Does God see us as "America the Beautiful" or, "America the Ugly"?

HOW DID WE GET HERE?

The Bible connects work (and therefore business) with family, peace and prosperity: "If anyone does not provide for his relatives, and especially for his immediate family, he has denied the faith and is worse than an unbeliever" (1 Tim. 5:8). Let's look at the trouble with business in America and connect the dots to trouble with the family and the poor.

Hyman Minsky's Model

Economist Hyman Minsky came up with a business model that included three levels of borrowing: hedge, speculative and Ponzi. Hedge and speculative were acceptable means of borrowing and would not create serious financial stress on a company. The Ponzi financing method would create distress in the financial system, if everyone used it.

"Ponzi financing" is when a business borrows money and cannot repay the loan from the investment made using the proceeds of the loan. The only way to keep repayments current is to sell purchased assets. America is doing exactly this: By issuing government debt. America prints money and then simply issues more debt to repay its loans.

America and her businesses have been involved in "Ponzi financing" by seeking short-term profits over long-term development of labor and production. Businesses that use the Ponzi method do not need a business plan, product, or market. Their plan is to sell assets as cash when needed for interest and principle payments. This is done for the profit of a few at the expense of the many.

Businesses that use Ponzi financing attract greedy people who only want to maximize profits today. They take as much as they can for themselves. **America's government and her related structure of entitlements is the largest Ponzi scheme ever concocted.** The government debt keeps increasing and America (Congress, the Treasury and the Federal Reserve) continually sells government debt (in other words, keep borrowing) to keep the scheme going.

If we had followed what the Founding Fathers intended in promoting "general Welfare," we would have invested in people and children, also known as "Posterity." This would have generated and per-petuated a strong working middle class, resulting in a "more perfect Union" and "domestic Tranquility." America did this until about 50 years ago.

Government, however well-intentioned in its inception, has resulted in the poor not having to take responsibility for themselves and their families. They don't have to work, they don't have to be concerned about who pays their medical bills and as a result, America is now bankrupt. It spends nearly $1 trillion on all types of entitle-ments to the poor.

America may have a total net worth of $80-100 trillion, but total debt — government debt and unfunded liabilities — amounts to **$140 trillion**. Someone may argue that one of these numbers is larger or smaller, so maybe our negative net worth is only $10 or 20 trillion. Same difference: **America is BROKE.** (figure 9, page 97)

A business is bankrupt if it cannot make payments to its credi-tors. It may have a positive net worth, but if it cannot pay its bills, then its creditors can throw the company into different levels of bankruptcy: Chapter 7, 11, or 13 bankruptcy.

America's monetary system, **the dollar**, is the reserve currency of the world. Therefore it can issue new debt with the push of a "magic but-ton." Once America's dollar is not recognized as the reserve currency of the world, America will find the **magic button** glued shut. (And what God glues shut, no one can unglue.)

America's Business & Social Failures

America's big businesses and government have worked together to do well for themselves. Their programs, however, have resulted in the destruction of its own long-term sustainability. As a result, America has lost her worldwide influence as well as any effectiveness in dealing with the world's economic, social, financial, as well as political troubles.

1. Losing Jobs Overseas

America is shipping production and jobs overseas. As a result, the financial future for the 60-75 million children who will become adults in the next decade is bleak at best. College will be a dead end.

Within the next seven years, 21 million college graduates will have only 10-12 million jobs available commensurate to their education. Paul Craig Roberts in his mind-blowing book, "The Failure of Laissez Faire Capitalism" has a horrifying calculation: "That leaves 8 million American university graduates over a 7-year period (2007-2014) chasing 1,434,000 jobs over a 10-year period (2008-2018)." Can college increase expectations and diminish hopes?

America's economic inequality is staggering. Surely this violates the intent of the Founding Fathers to create a "**more perfect Union**" as well as provide blessings of liberty and freedom for the 50 million in poverty. They do not feel blessed and have no liberty, unless someone wants to define liberty as "free to stand in line" for their next government handout.

2. Rich Ruling Over the Poor

"The rich rule over the poor, and the borrower is servant to the lender." (Proverbs 22:7)

The rich are getting richer and the poor are getting poorer.

The rich are using the financial crisis that they created to further their own power and control the world's poor. They make like they care and are helping, but it is as the Japanese say "shibai" (fake). "Economist Michael Hudson calls it *'financialized neofeudalism'*: People are being enserfed and economies destroyed all in order that bankers don't have to suffer losses on their casino gambling bets."

("The Failure of Laissez Faire Capitalism & Economic Dissolution of the West, by Paul Craig Roberts, 2013)

They make large bets to enrich themselves. Like my ole Vegas days, only thing I had to pay for were my losses. Banks today are too big to fail, so they scoop their wins, and pass off their losses.

3. Healthcare Costs Devastating the Working Class

Medical costs are skyrocketing for many reasons:
1. We are living longer.
2. Corporations are developing drugs that are curing diseases. These are huge money-makers. Some believe this is part of the big money that influences government for profit.
3. No one disputes the effectiveness of medicine when they themselves or someone they know are cured. I am not dealing with the righteousness of medicine.
4. However, it seems that the extra costs of living an additional five years are exorbitant.
5. The poor and homeless have the same medical costs.

4. Welfare State Disabling & Enabling

The welfare state mentality has disabled 100-150 million Americans (of 310 million) by enabling them. Government and its bureaucracy has won favor, and votes, but costs have been HUGE. A classic quote says, "The American Republic will endure until the day Congress discovers it can bribe the public with the public's money."

Regarding this anonymous quote, Wikipedia says, "...Two centuries ago, a somewhat obscure Scotsman named Tyler made this profound observation: 'A democracy cannot exist as a permanent form of government. It can only exist until the majority discovers it can vote itself largess out of the public treasury. After that, the majority always votes for the candidate promising the most benefits with the result the democracy collapses because of the loose fiscal policy ensuing, always to be followed by a dictatorship, then a monarchy.'"

Regardless of the author, it perfectly describes America today: The political candidate who promises the most, wins. The Bible confirms: "For the time will come when men will not put up with sound doctrine. Instead, to suit their own desires, they will gather around them a great number of teachers to say what their itching ears want to hear. They will turn their ears away from the truth and turn aside to myths" (2 Tim. 4:3-4).

> *"In the course of time, Absalom provided himself with a chariot and horses and with fifty men to run ahead of him. He would get up early and stand by the side of the road leading to the city gate. Whenever anyone came with a complaint to be placed before the king for a decision, Absalom would call out to him, 'What town are you from?' He would answer, 'Your servant is from one of the tribes of Israel.' Then Absalom would say to him, 'Look, your claims are valid and proper, but there is no representative of the king to hear you.' And Absalom would add, 'If only I were appointed judge in the land! Then everyone who has a complaint or case could come to me and I would see that he gets justice.'"* (2 Samuel 15:1-4)

Absalom lived 3,000 years too early; were he alive today, he'd be President of the United States.

5. The Biggest "Kick the Can" Game Ever: Social Programs (figure 10, page 98)

Social Security and Medicaid have unfunded liabilities of over $100 trillion (The Washington Post, "Does the United States have $128 trillion in unfunded liabilities?", Glenn Kessler, October 23, 2013). These are future costs that exceed the ability of current cash value to fund.

The government has continued to "kick the can" of debt down the road. No one wants to pay the piper as long as they get "theirs" today. This short-sighted, short-term lack of concern for others is exactly what is wrong with our current government.

6. Poor Dollar = Poor People

The government deficit spending and related Federal Reserve money creation has weakened the dollar over the past 50 years. Here are some price changes:

ITEM	PRICE in 60s	PRICE TODAY (2012-2014)
1. Milk (gallon)	$.93	$4.00
2. Apartment (2 BR, N.Y. Wash Sq.)	$250/month	$4,500/month
3. Subway (N.Y.)	$.15 (roundtrip)	$2.50 (One way, anywhere)
4. Coca Cola	$.14	$.50-1.00 (depending)
5. Minimum Wage	$1.15/hour	$8.00/hour
6. Gas (gallon)	$.25	$4.00
7. Cigarettes (pack in N.Y.)	$1.60	$12
8. Mustang	$2,320	$22,500
9. Kellogg's Corn Flakes (12 oz.)	$.25	$3.79
10. Campbell's Tomato Soup (can)	$.11	$1.09
11. McDonald's hamburger	$.15	$1.00
12. Oreos	$.43 (12 oz.)	$4.49 (14.3 oz)

Sources:

1. CBS New York (1/17/2014) (http://newyork.cbslocal.com/top-lists/the-price-of-living-from-1964-to-2014)

2. FOOD PRICES (Items 9-12) Food Timeline library (http://www.foodtimeline.org/foodfaq5.html#usaprices)

An interesting site on the Bureau of Labor Statistics (http://www.bls.gov/data/inflation_calculator.htm) features a **CPI Inflation Calculator**. It confirms what we see from the prices in the above chart: **One dollar in 1964 could buy as much as $7.64 can buy in 2014**. (figure 11, page 99)

The dollar has been on a steady decline (read: loss of purchasing power also called "inflation"). Each group of people is affected differently. Those with well-paying jobs in strong industries are able to keep up. The sad part of inflation is its impact on the elderly who retired 20 or 30 years ago. They find it difficult at best. Living on fixed incomes forces them to keep expenses inhumanely low, damaging their souls. A true travesty!

COMING COLLAPSE OF THE DOLLAR?

A possible trigger for the dollar's collapse may be any of the following: (However, there are many more possible options not yet evident on the horizon and therefore unpredictable.)

1. Petrodollar Failure

The dollar is the reserve currency of the world. Over 80% of the world's total transactions are paid using the United States dollar. (moneynews.com, "China's Yuan Eclipses Euro in World Trade. Next Target: US Dollar?" 04 Dec 2013, John Morgan)

Any significant shift from the dollar as reserve currency for international transactions will have serious implications for its collapse. This could very possibly start with oil purchases. What cannot be predicted is whether it would happen slowly or accelerate into a "Minsky Moment" (sudden major collapse). Consequently, should this happen it would have serious implications on inflation, interest rates on U.S. debt, and the bond market.

In simple language, **America will be "in deep kim chee!"**

2. The U.S. Government Bond: The Ugly Duckling of World Currencies

The United States is feeding itself off the fumes of the government paper it is printing. The national debt is over $18 trillion. They've borrowed from the world nearly $6 trillion in government paper bonds, notes, and bills. Our government borrowed from itself. Wouldn't it be nice if you could borrow from yourself? (figure 12, page 99)

Our own Federal Reserve balance sheet has ballooned from approximately $2 trillion to $4.2 trillion in government paper holdings. The government borrowed from its own Federal Reserve. (It is forced to do so because the rest of the world recently refused to keep buying, or they've demanded higher interest rates.) The Federal Reserve purchased the debt through its **Quantum Easing Programs**.

What happens when the music stops and the world demands higher interest rates? How much paper can the Federal Reserve keep buying? Is anyone looking?

Sadly, no.

Our government has also unbelievably borrowed from our own **Social Security Trust Fund (SSTF)**, with assets of approximately $2.8 trillion (in 2013). They do this by "selling debt" to the SSTF.

Do you mean to say the cash is gone?

Not to worry; SSTF is holding $2.8 trillion in government debt, and of course we know our government would never default on that debt... Right?! *Hmmm....*

3. Financial Attack: B.R.I.C. or Mideast?

It's possible that Brazil, Russia, India, China (also known as B.R.I.C. nations) or a Mideast country could launch an all-out attack on the United States. Of course, this would happen only if they were unhappy with us, right? Do they have any reason? *Hmmm....*

This attack won't be with bombs, rockets, or chemical weapons; that would be suicide for them. America is still too strong militarily for that type of war. But a **financial attack**, an attack on our bond market or on the dollar? You may wonder, *How would this happen?*

Most likely from an unlikely angle, a strategy that no one can now see. It may involve gold as the backing of our currency. All central banks hold gold to back currency, yet all play along that gold is a relic without investment value. (figure 13, page 100)

Yet the world may shudder when they see the next release of gold figures: **How much gold does China hold?** China held approximately 1,000 tons of gold at the last release (circa 2007). However, people tracking China's gold production and net imports think it may have as much as **7,500 tons of gold**. Why is this significant? **America only holds about 8,000 tons of gold**.

Could China be making a move to replace the U.S. dollar as the world's reserve currency?

That would be a huge blow to America.

4. Rising Interest Rates

The world banking system is holding approximately $18 trillion of U.S. debt. Current interest rates on the 10-year bond is approximately 2.5%. This is far below the historic norm purely because the Federal Reserve along with the powers-in-control wanted to save America.

Regardless, the interest rates will eventually be corrected and go up. When they do, America may end up paying much more for the money it borrowed.

If we use the $18 trillion figure for government debt, and interest rates return to a nominal historic rate (say 6.5% for 30-year bonds), America would be paying an additional **$720 billion** just for interest. ($18 trillion x (6.5% - 2.5%= 4%), therefore, $18 trillion x 4% = $720 billion.) (figure 14, page 100)

This does not include additional deficit from the impact of rising rates. Bottom line: Bad for economy, bad for tax revenues, and total deficits easily at $2 trillion a year. Bad for America.

5. Healthcare/ ObamaCare: America's Tipping Point?

ObamaCare's current projected annual cost (which has steadily been increasing) is now $260 billion. Who's to say it doesn't double 5-10 years from now? At what point will the dollar break? (figure 15, page 101)

America may have as many as **60-80 million receiving medical care** that the other **160 million** citizens must somehow pay for.

These national medical costs are fast-approaching a tipping point and will break the backs of Americans carrying its costs. If this was the only expense, America might be able to bear the burden. But along with all the other troubled social programs, America is headed for disaster, and soon.

Does anyone know the true costs of ObamaCare? Could ObamaCare add a trillion dollars a year to our already escalating deficit? Worse, will this create an entitlement attitude?

The good thing about Hawaii is it takes care of its people. It has one of the best medical systems in the United States. The bad thing about Hawaii is it takes so good care of its people, that even if they have no income (homeless or poor with no job) they still take care of them. I'm not saying they shouldn't, I'm saying the costs are borne by the rest of us who have incomes.

Homeless in Hawaii who require medical attention (including for non-serious ailments, e.g. fevers or headaches) just call 911. Ambulances arrive to give first-class service. Once in the hospital, costs can run $5,000 to $10,000. The good thing about Hawaii, is it has Aloha Medical Care. The bad thing is the cost of aloha.

6. World Geo-Political Struggles

America has lost her influence in the world. The cause is difficult to pinpoint, but I believe it goes back to God: America's leaders are not men of character. The Bible tells us to pray for our leaders, and I do, but that doesn't mean we cannot make reasoned analysis about the state of our nation. Many of our leaders tell us they are religious or believe in God, but seem to redefine belief. Essentially, they act as if they do not believe in God.

America's policies seem to flip-flop based on polls or what is in line with the powerbrokers. The Bible calls these leaders "fools," and God frustrates "fools," to neutralize them on the world scene. As a result, many geo-political situations are headed for disaster or at the very least, a giant mess:

A. Invasion of Iraq: America gave back in a few short months what it took 10 years to secure.

B. Russia's invasion of Crimea: America's strategy seems to be "We'll spank your pocketbook and revoke your passports." A strategy of appeasement?

C. Nuclear Iran: "Playdate" and stalemate negotiations will soon lead to a nuclear Iran.

D. Trouble in Syria, Egypt, Libya, and Nigeria: America seems absolutely confused.

E. Nuclear North Korea

F. Islamic extremism worldwide (including Taliban, Al Qaeda and I.S.I.S.): American's strategy seems to be, "Make friends so they won't be mad at us." Completely ineffective.

G. Trouble in Israel and Palestinians in Gaza: America has only been a nuisance and non-entity in helping mediate a ceasefire.

WHAT DOES THE "END GAME" LOOK LIKE?

No one can know the timing but what is certain is that the global picture will end badly for most. Like the 2008-2009 financial melt-down, most of the powers-in-control know something is up. But as long as it doesn't happen today, they can keep kicking the can down the road. Lest we be too harsh on them, remember one of the greatest, godliest kings, Hezekiah, who failed because of his selfishness:

> "Then Isaiah said to Hezekiah, 'Hear the word of the Lord: The time will surely come when everything in your palace, and all that your fathers have stored up until this day, will be carried off to Babylon. Nothing will be left, says the Lord. And some of your descendants, your own flesh and blood, that will be born to you, will be taken away, and they will become eunuchs in the palace of the king of Babylon.' 'The word of the Lord you have spoken is good,' Hezekiah replied. **For he thought, 'Will there not be peace and security in my lifetime?'**" (2 Kings 20:16-19, emphasis added)

One of the brightest global thinkers in the world today is John Mauldin. He has a broad range of research covering financial, economic, geo-political and social arenas. He is not overly fatalistic, conservative, or liberal in his views; he maintains a balanced approach. He has a website, Mauldin Economic, that I encourage you to check out. An excerpt from a June 14, 2014 article:

"The Age of Transformation—The Second Wave of Transformation"

"Similar challenges are already developing throughout Europe and in Japan and China, and will probably hit the United States by the end of this decade. While each country will deal with its own crisis differently, these crises are going to severely impact social structures and economies not just nationally but globally. Taken together, I think these emerging developments will be bigger in scope and impact than the credit crisis of 2008.

"While each country's crisis may seemingly have a different cause, the problems stem largely from the inability of governments to pay for promised retirement and health benefits while meeting all the other obligations of government. Whether that inability is due to demographic problems, fiscal irresponsibility, unduly high tax burdens, sclerotic labor laws, or a lack of growth due to bureaucratic restraints, the results will be the same. Debts are going to have to be 'rationalized' (an economic euphemism for **default**), and promises are going to have to be painfully adjusted. The adjustments will not seem fair and will give rise to a great deal of societal Sturm und Drang [storm and stress], but at the end of the process I believe the world will be much better off. Going through the coming period is, however, going to be challenging.

"'How did you go bankrupt?' asked Hemingway's protagonist. 'Gradually,' was the answer, 'and then all at once.' European governments are going bankrupt gradually, and then we will have that infamous *Bang!* moment when it seems to happen all at once. Bond markets will rebel, interest rates will skyrocket, and governments will be unable to meet their obligations. Japan is trying to forestall their moment with the most breathtaking quantitative easing scheme in the history of the world, electing to devalue their currency as the primary way to cope. The U.S. has a window of time in which it will still be possible to deal with its problems (and I am hopeful that we can), but without structural reform of our entitlement programs we will go the way of Europe and numerous other countries before us."

"...This breaking wave of economic changes will not be

the end of the world, of course – one way or another we'll survive. But **how you, your family, and your businesses are positioned to deal with the crisis** will have a great deal to do with the manner in which you survive. We are not just cogs in a vast machine turning to powers we cannot control. If we **properly prepare**, we can do more than merely 'survive.' But achieving that means you're going to have to rely more on your own resources and ingenuity and less on governments. If you find yourself in a position where you are dependent upon the government for your personal situation, you might not be happy." (John Mauldin website, 6/14/14, "Thoughts from the Frontline")

In general, human nature works against planning now for inevitable disaster. People with symptoms of cancer don't go to the doctor until it's too late. People with large credit card debt (with interest at 18%) keep charging their credit cards rather than sell the second car or house and adjust spending. Most professionals in the financial markets could foresee the sub-prime problem, but few did anything about it (except Morgan Stanley who shorted the market and made a killing).

To say this will end badly is to overlook that it has already ended badly for most in America.

GOD HAS A PLAN: BRINGING AMERICA TO HER KNEES

God has a plan to work for the good of America's families. It might not look good right now. But eyesight is a bad way to gauge our future, since most of us drive by looking in the rear view mirror (myself included). Let's look at what God's plan might be through His prophet Hosea:

> "…Their deeds do not permit them to return to their God. A spirit of prostitution is in their heart; they do not acknowledge the Lord.…

They are unfaithful to the Lord; they give birth to illegitimate children." (Hosea 5:4, 7)

*"...Ephraim will be laid waste on the **day of reckoning**. Among the tribes of Israel I proclaim what is certain. Judah's leaders are like those who move boundary stones. I will pour out my wrath on them like a flood of water....For I will be like a lion to Ephraim, like a great lion to Judah. I will tear them to pieces and go away; I will carry them off, with no one to rescue them. Then I will go back to my place until they admit their guilt. And they will seek my face; in their misery they will earnestly seek me."* (Hosea 5:9-10, 14-15)

Israel had been disobedient. God warned He would discipline them. He sent destruction like a lion to the people. When they hit rock bottom and admitted their guilt in abandoning Him, He blessed them again.

America has been disobedient; she has turned from God. We the people have turned away from our God-given responsibility when He gave this great nation: The people were to remain connected to government by electing and selecting those who lead our country. Only then would we the people be able to secure the rights given to us by our Creator, God.

God is orchestrating pain and suffering for America. We as a nation will end up poor and manifest as the five groups of poor. However, God can cause all things to work together for good. Which means that **when America hits rock bottom and the people return to their Creator, God will heal our land**.

Figure 1. Brady Guista

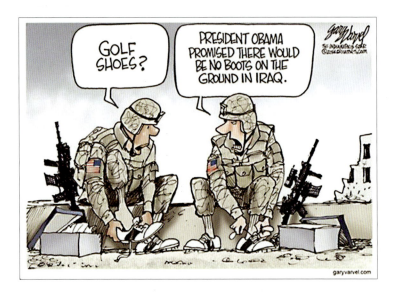

Figure 2. Boots on the Ground

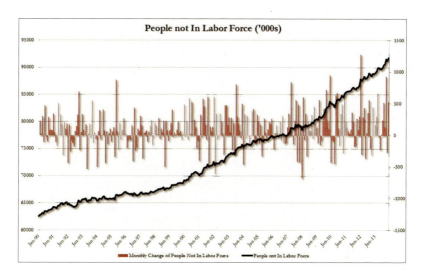

Figure 3. People Not In Labor Force

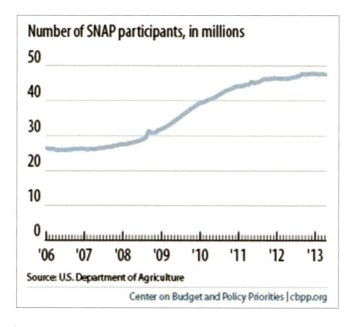

Figure 4. People on Food Stamps

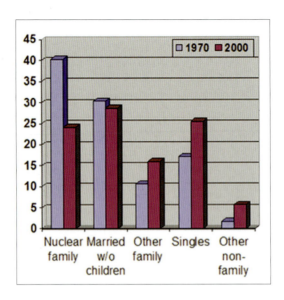

Figure 5. Nuclear Family

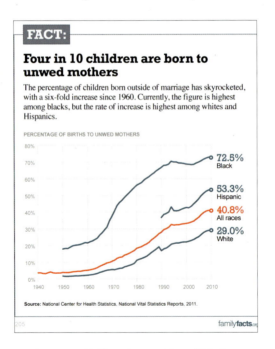

Figure 6. Children Born to Unwed Mothers

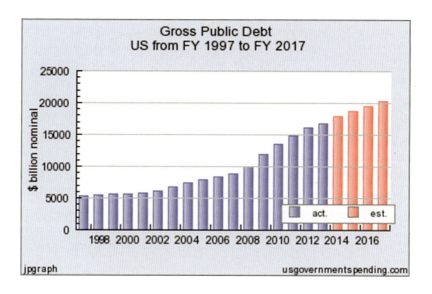

Figure 7. US Debt Chart

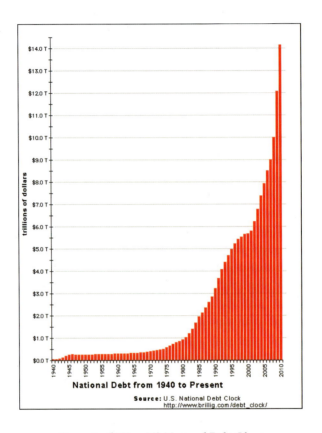

Figure 8. 50 Year US National Debt Chart

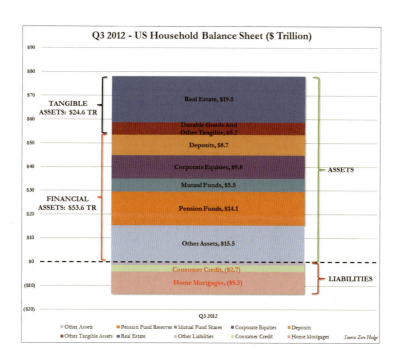

Figure 9. Assets US Households

Figure 10. Kick the Can

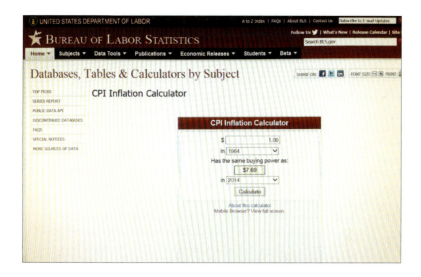

Figure 11. Bureau of Labor Statistics Inflation Calculator

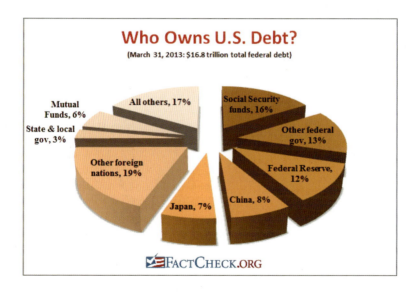

Figure 12. Debt Pie Chart, Who Owns US Debt

Table 1: Top 40 reported official gold holdings (as at December 2012)

		Tonnes	% of reserves			Tonnes	% of reserves
1	United States	8,133.5	76%	21	Austria	280.0	55%
2	Germany	3,391.3	73%	22	Belgium	227.5	39%
3	IMF	2,814.0	-	23	Philippines	192.7	12%
4	Italy	2,451.8	72%	24	Algeria	173.6	5%
5	France	2,435.4	71%	25	Thailand	152.4	4%
6	China	1,054.1	2%	26	Singapore	127.4	3%
7	Switzerland	1,040.1	11%	27	Sweden	125.7	13%
8	Russia	957.8	9%	28	South Africa	125.1	13%
9	Japan	765.2	3%	29	Mexico	124.5	4%
10	Netherlands	612.5	60%	30	Libya	116.6	5%
11	India	557.7	10%	31	BIS	116.0	-
12	ECB	502.1	33%	32	Kazakhstan	115.3	22%
13	Taiwan	423.6	6%	33	Greece	111.9	82%
14	Portugal	382.5	90%	34	Romania	103.7	12%
15	Venezuela	365.8	75%	35	Poland	102.9	5%
16	Turkey	359.6	16%	36	Korea	84.4	1%
17	Saudi Arabia	322.9	3%	37	Australia	79.9	9%
18	United Kingdom	310.3	16%	38	Kuwait	79.0	13%
19	Lebanon	286.8	29%	39	Egypt	75.6	25%
20	Spain	281.6	30%	40	Indonesia	73.1	4%

For information on the methodology behind this data, as well as footnotes for specific countries, please see our table of Latest World Official Gold Reserves, at http://www.gold.org/government_affairs/gold_reserves/

Source: IMF, World Gold Council

Figure 13. Gold Holdings, Central Banks World

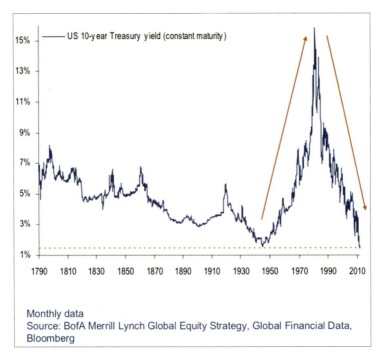

Monthly data
Source: BofA Merrill Lynch Global Equity Strategy, Global Financial Data, Bloomberg

Figure 14. 10-year Treasury

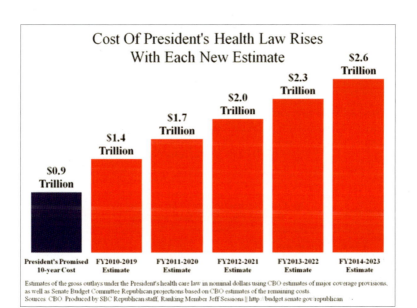

Figure 15. Obama Care Annual Cost Projections

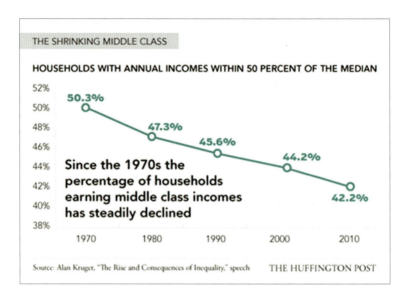

Figure 16. Middle Class Household Income

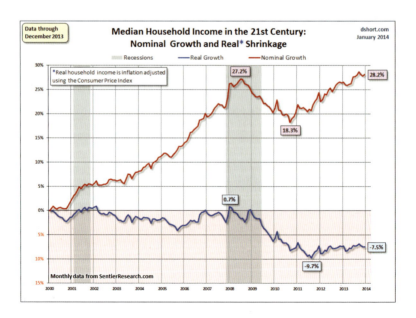

Figure 17. Middle Class Household Income

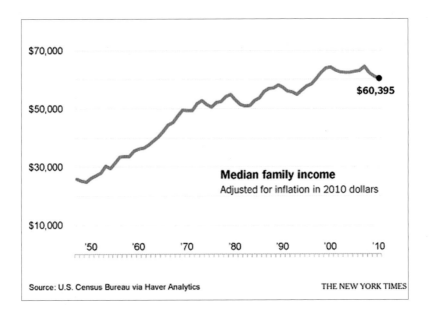

Figure 18. Middle Class Household Income

Figure 19. Real average earnings have not increased in 50 years

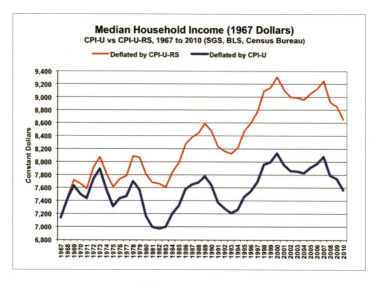

Figure 20. Middle Class Household Income Constant

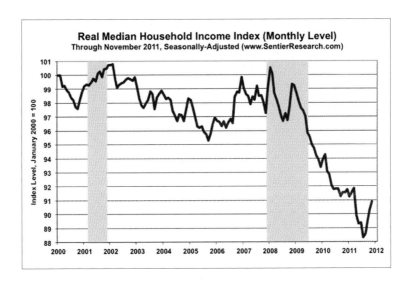

Figure 21. Real Median Income

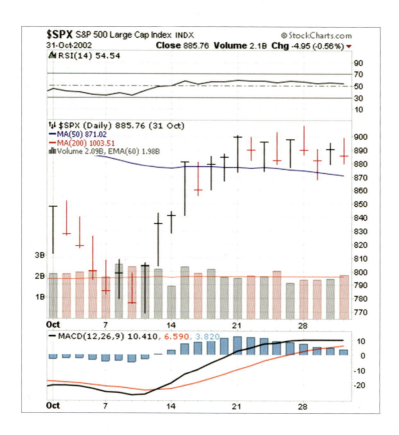

Figure 22. SPX Oct 2002 A1 Hedge Crash

CHAPTER 4

WHAT IS GOD THINKING?

"Therefore, I urge you, brothers, in view of God's mercy,
to offer your bodies as living sacrifices, holy and pleasing to God
— this is your spiritual act of worship.
Do not conform any longer to the pattern of this world,
but be transformed by the renewing of your mind.
Then you will be able to test and approve what God's will is
— his good, pleasing and perfect will."
(Romans 12:1-2)

GOD'S THOUGHTS THROUGH HIS WORD

In the modern Christian classic, "Experiencing God," author Henry Blackaby wrote: "When you want to know what God is doing around you, pray. Watch to see what happens next. Make the connection between your prayer and ensuing events....Be ready to make whatever adjustments are required to **join God in what He is doing.**"

Simply, figuring out what God wants you to do means figuring out what He is thinking. It also means looking around to see what He is doing, and following Him. Also, it would be foolish to try to guess what God is thinking without His Word. **We know God's thoughts through His Word**.

Let's explore how God's Truths apply to people in the "poor" groups and in our nation. And I leave it to you to see if it fits the people and situations in your life.

GOD'S THOUGHTS & DESIRES FOR AMERICA

America may very well be the most blessed nation in the history of the world. At one time we had the highest standard of living in the world. America fit the model for blessing that God lays out in His Word:

"If you fully obey the Lord your God and carefully follow all his commands I give you today, the Lord your God will set you high above all the nations on earth. 2 All these blessings will come upon you and accompany you if you obey the Lord your God:

3 You will be blessed in the city and blessed in the country.

4 The fruit of your womb will be blessed, and the crops of your land and the young of your livestock — the calves of your herds and the lambs of your flocks.

5 Your basket and your kneading trough will be blessed.

6 You will be blessed when you come in and blessed when you go out.

7 The Lord will grant that the enemies who rise up against you will be defeated before you. They will come at you from one direction but flee from you in seven.

8 The Lord will send a blessing on your barns and on everything you put your hand to. The Lord your God will bless you in the land he is giving you...

12 The Lord will open the heavens, the storehouse of his bounty, to send rain on your land in season and to bless all the work of your hands. You will lend to many nations but will borrow from none."

(Deuteronomy 28:1-8, 12)

God spoke to Israel through Moses and laid out a model for blessings and curses. Blessings resulted from obedience to His commands, and curses from disobedience. This is a basic principle God lays out for all of His people. The same is applicable to America.

America has surely been blessed:

1. In the 20th century, our nation saw a rapid expansion in our cities and across the country like never before: our interstate highway system, bridges, nationwide electric grid, excellent water and sewer systems for our modern cities, excellent communities in the suburbs, to list a few.

2. Our educational system was one of the best in the world, and produced some of the brightest, most creative young adults in engineering, business, medicine, science, technology, and many more areas.

3. Our nation has "some of the richest agricultural land in the world. Even more important, it was land with superb system of navigable rivers that allowed the country's agricultural surplus to be shipped to world markets, creating a class of businessmen-farmers that is unique in history." ("The Next Hundred Years," George Friedman, Doubleday, NY, p. 40)

4. America was instrumental in winning WWI and WWII and was the peacekeeper of the world.

5. America was a major lender to the rest of the world. Now it is the largest borrower in the world. (Wikipedia, List of Countries by External Debt, 2014)

6. America has been the greatest sender of missionaries in history. In 2013 it sent 127,000 missionaries. (ChristianityToday.org 7/29/13, "The World's Top Missionary-Sending Country Will Surprise You")

7. America has been the greatest giver to the world in the history of the world. It has given $2.6 trillion in the past 50 years in foreign

aid (measured in 2006 dollars). (Journal of Economic Perspectives, vol. 22, #2, Spring 2008, by William Easterly & Tobias Pfutze, p. 29)

God also issued a warning, directly following the list of blessings came the curses of disobedience:

"However, if you do not obey the Lord your God and do not carefully follow all his commands and decrees I am giving you today, all these curses will come upon you and overtake you:

16 You will be cursed in the city and cursed in the country.

17 Your basket and your kneading trough will be cursed.

18 The fruit of your womb will be cursed, and the crops of your land, and the calves of your herds and the lambs of your flocks.

19 You will be cursed when you come in and cursed when you go out.

20 The Lord will send on you curses, confusion and rebuke in everything you put your hand to, until you are destroyed and come to sudden ruin because of the evil you have done in forsaking him. 21 The Lord will plague you with diseases until he has destroyed you from the land you are entering to possess. 22 The Lord will strike you with wasting disease, with fever and inflammation, with scorching heat and drought, with blight and mildew, which will plague you until you perish. 23 The sky over your head will be bronze, the ground beneath you iron. 24 The Lord will turn the rain of your country into dust and powder; it will come down from the skies until you are destroyed.

25 The Lord will cause you to be defeated before your enemies." (Deuteronomy 28:15-25)

Furthermore (in a fast-following Scripture):

"The alien who lives among you will rise above you higher and higher, but you will sink lower and lower. He will lend to you, but you will not lend to him. He will be the head, but you will be the tail." (Deuteronomy 28:43-44)

GOD IS ANGRY WITH AMERICA
& WITHDRAWS HIS FAVOR

Notice I wrote earlier: "At one time we had the highest standard of living in the world." We may still have a decent rating by world standards but we are in dire decline. American is now ranked ninth in Gross Domestic Product per capita (and probably falling fast). (Wikipedia, List of countries by GDP per capita)

1. Most of our major cities have slums, abandoned houses and buildings, and poverty in the streets in the form of homelessness.

2. Our educational system is no longer among the world's top. (National Public Radio, "U.S. Students Slide in Global Ranking on Math, Reading, Science," by Bill Chappell, 12/3/13)

3. Our agricultural system is still productive but we have a severe nationwide drought.

4. America is no longer winning wars. Vietnam was the first major conflict where America lost. We stumbled in Iraq, Afghanistan, and in the latest pullout from Iraq (December 2011). Iraq now seems a loss for the 10-year war effort. The ISIS takeover and establishment of their caliphate is decimating for America. America is losing recent wars against much smaller forces because we've forsaken God.

5. America used to lend to the world nations, now we are its biggest borrower with government debt over $18 trillion. United Kingdom is second at $10 trillion with Germany at $5.7 trillion. (Wikipedia, List of countries by external debt)

GOD IS SOVEREIGN & IN ACTIVE CONTROL

In the Old Testament, God speaks to individuals but He also speaks to nations. In fact, He brings discipline on nations, or groups of people, to either get them back on track or to be an example to others. He also uses other nations to bring discipline upon Israel, including

Egypt, Babylon, Assyria, and Persia. In this passage, God spoke to Israel and makes reference to King Cyrus of Persia *"to fulfill His purpose"*:

> *"Listen to me, O house of Jacob, all you who remain of the house of Israel.... Fix it in mind, take it to heart, you rebels. Remember the former things, those of long ago; I am God, and there is no other; I am God, and there is none like me. I make known the end from the beginning, from ancient times, what is still to come. I say: My purpose will stand, and I will do all that I please. From the east I summon a bird of prey; from a far-off land, a man **to fulfill my purpose**. What I have said, that will I bring about; what I have planned, that will I do. Listen to me, you stubborn-hearted, you who are far from righteousness. **I am bringing my righteousness near, it is not far away; and my salvation will not be delayed.**"* (Isaiah 46:8-13)

God is actively involved in nations. He is not passively sitting around, crossing His fingers, hoping the nations do the right thing. God is sovereign still.

GOD'S THOUGHTS & DESIRES FOR NATIONS

As God was actively involved in the past, so is He actively involved today. More importantly (for this book), **God is actively involved in America**. America was granted God's blessings for her first 200 years. But in the last 50 years, America strayed. So, God is bringing curses (discipline) to this country.

Jesus establishes a foundational principle of discipline (cross reference Deut. 28, aforementioned):

> *"Peter asked, 'Lord, are you telling this parable to us, or to everyone?' The Lord answered, 'Who then is the faithful and wise manager, whom the master puts in charge of his servants to give them*

their food allowance at the proper time? It will be good for that servant whom the master finds doing so when he returns. I tell you the truth, he will put him in charge of all his possessions. But suppose the servant says to himself, 'My master is taking a long time in coming,' and he then begins to beat the menservants and maidservants and to eat and drink and get drunk. The master of that servant will come on a day when he does not expect him and at an hour he is not aware of. He will cut him to pieces and assign him a place with the unbelievers.'That servant who knows his master's will and does not get ready or does not do what his master wants will be beaten with many blows. But the one who does not know and does things deserving punishment will be beaten with few blows. From everyone who has been given much, much will be demanded; and from the one who has been entrusted with much, much more will be asked.'" (Luke 12:41-48)

When Peter asked the Lord if this teaching was just for them or for everyone, Jesus' reply made it clear: It is for everyone. Therefore, we must ask ourselves, **Are we (America) the good and faithful manager or the unwise and abusive servant?**

America has been blessed more than any other country in the world. God entrusted much to America because He had a great plan for her. Part of the plan was to be peacemaker and protector of the world, as well as a light to the world. Though the U.S. still is a force for good (e.g. sending missionaries) we have fallen far short. God doesn't average our good works with our wickedness.

God disciplines whole nations when they go astray:

"Again the anger of the Lord burned against Israel, and he incited David against them, saying, 'Go and take a census of Israel and Judah.' ...So the Lord sent a plague on Israel from that morning

until the end of the time designated, and seventy thousand of the people from Dan to Beersheba died." (2 Samuel 24:1, 15)

God was angry with Israel; He had entrusted her with much and she did not steward it well. So He orchestrated events to have David (through Satan, 1 Chron. 21:1) take a census of Israel. Although census had been taken before, God knew David was getting proud so He used David to bring discipline on Israel and 70,000 died.

God is doing the same to America.

GOD IS ANGRY WITH THE WORLD: ARE WE THAT CLOSE?

One more verse to reveal God's thoughts and shed light on what He's up to:

> *"Therefore wait ye upon me, saith the Lord, until the day that I rise up to the prey: for my determination is to gather the nations, that I may assemble the kingdoms, to pour upon them mine indignation, even all my fierce anger: for all the earth shall be devoured with the fire of my jealousy."* (Zephaniah 3:8, KJV)

The challenge with the Scriptures is understanding the context, intent, timing, and audience the prophet was addressing. For answers, we turn to the professionals, trusted commentators:

Albert Barnes' Notes on the Bible (Albert Barnes Notes, published Blackie & Son, London, 1884-85-from Barnes' Notes, Electronic Database Copyright © 1997, 2003, 2005, 2006 by Biblesoft, Inc.)

1. The day is probably in the first instance, the deliverance from Babylon. But the words seem to be purposely enlarged, that they may embrace other judgments of God also.
2. For the words *"to gather the nations, assemble the kingdoms,"* describe some array of nations against God and His people; gathering them-

selves for their own end at that time, but, in His purpose, gathering themselves for their own destruction, rather than the mere tranquil reunion of those of different nations in the city of Babylon, when the Medes and Persians came against them. Nor again are they altogether fulfilled in the destruction of Jerusalem, or any other event until now.

3. In its fullest sense the prophecy seems to belong to the same events in the last struggle of Anti-Christ....

4. The outpouring of all God's wrath, the devouring of the whole earth, in the fullest sense of the words, belongs to the end of the world, when He shall say to the wicked, "Depart from Me, ye cursed, into everlasting fire."

5. The Church, having sinned, had to "wait" for a while "*for God*" who by His Providence withdrew Himself, yet at last delivered it.

J. Vernon McGee puts it this way: "This earth which you and I are living on is moving toward a judgment. Although folk don't believe it, they are moving to judgment. It is this judgment which will be initiated when the Lord Jesus Christ returns to this earth for His church. It begins then with the Great Tribulation period and ends when He comes to establish His Kingdom on this earth." ("Through the Bible," J. Vernon McGee, Thomas Nelson Publishers, Nashville, Tennessee)

Essentially God is saying: **We are marching towards a Day of Judgment**. God has been patient, but His patience is limited. He tells us through Zephaniah of the coming Day; closer now than ever before in history. The closer we get to that Day, the worse the world will be, and those who are poor and in poverty will be significantly impacted.

GOD'S THOUGHTS FOR THE POOR

Why does God love the poor? Does He love the poor more than those who are not poor? How do we reconcile the fact that the Bible says

God loves everyone — rich or poor, hungry or full, generous or greedy, saved or unsaved? Because He wants all to come to know Jesus:

> *"Brothers, think of what you were when you were called. Not many of you were wise by human standards; not many were influential; not many were of noble birth. But God chose the foolish things of the world to shame the wise; God chose the weak things of the world to shame the strong. He chose the lowly things of this world and the despised things — and the things that are not — to nullify the things that are, so that no one may boast before him. It is because of him that you are in Christ Jesus, who has become for us wisdom from God — that is, our righteousness, holiness and redemption. Therefore, as it is written: 'Let him who boasts boast in the Lord.'"* (1 Corinthians 1:26-31)

> *"Listen, my dear brothers: Has not God chosen those who are poor in the eyes of the world to be **rich in faith** and to inherit the kingdom he promised those who love him? But you have insulted the poor. Is it not the rich who are exploiting you? Are they not the ones who are dragging you into court? Are they not the ones who are slandering the noble name of him to whom you belong?"* (James 2:5-7)

The poor are rich in faith. Yet despised by many. The homeless and those living in public housing are not treated the same as the well-dressed wealthy. They're often slighted when they stand in line with their EBT cards (Electronic Benefit Transfer or "food stamps"). They get disparaging looks and less-than treatment when trying to get medical care through Medicaid. God sees all and feels their pain.

They are also thankful for God's provisions. They have many problems and issues, but one thing sets them apart: The poor know more than anyone else that they need God to get to the next meal, next day, next appointment, next shower, and everything else in life. They know a great need for God.

GOD LOVES THE POOR

The best picture that clearly captures Christ's compassion for the poor is from Jesus' own words (an overflow of His heart):

> *"'For I was hungry and you gave me something to eat, I was thirsty and you gave me something to drink, I was a stranger and you invited me in, I needed clothes and you clothed me, I was sick and you looked after me, I was in prison and you came to visit me.' Then the righteous will answer him, 'Lord, when did we see you hungry and feed you, or thirsty and give you something to drink? When did we see you a stranger and invite you in, or needing clothes and clothe you? When did we see you sick or in prison and go to visit you?' The King will reply, 'I tell you the truth, whatever you did for one of the least of these brothers of mine, you did for me.'"*
> (Matthew 25:35-40)

Jesus loves those who are hungry, thirsty, strangers, needing clothes, sick and those in prison. Jesus says this group of people is special to Him: Whatever we do for them, we do for Him; and when we don't do anything for the poor, we do nothing for Jesus.

My problem with living out my Christianity was a lot like eating at a buffet line: I only took what I liked. In other words, I only live out the Jesus that I enjoy. God knew that so He started developing my paradigm for the poor long ago with Diana's family in 1963. He also had to connect me with Salvation Army (1995), Teen Challenge (1996), Tom Bauer and STN (1999). He even "tricked" me further to get me to Hawaii Cedar Church (2007) and Cedar Assembly of God (2010). That's a long journey! But it shows God's grace in being patient with me, knowing how slow I am to catch on. (***Thank you, Lord!***)

WHEN WE DON'T CARE FOR THE POOR, GOD DISCIPLINES US

Many things in the Bible are difficult to understand. However, what angers God is not one of them. That's very clear! And one of the worst violations is when we do not obey Him in caring for the poor:

"Shout it aloud, do not hold back. Raise your voice like a trumpet. Declare to my people their rebellion and to the house of Jacob their sins. For day after day they seek me out; they seem eager to know my ways, as if they were a nation that does what is right and has not forsaken the commands of its God. They ask me for just decisions and seem eager for God to come near them. 'Why have we fasted,' they say, 'and you have not seen it? Why have we humbled ourselves, and you have not noticed?' Yet on the day of your fasting, you do as you please and exploit all your workers. Your fasting ends in quarreling and strife, and in striking each other with wicked fists. You cannot fast as you do today and expect your voice to be heard on high. Is this the kind of fast I have chosen, only a day for a man to humble himself? Is it only for bowing one's head like a reed and for lying on sackcloth and ashes? Is that what you call a fast, a day acceptable to the Lord?

*"Is not this the kind of fasting I have chosen: to loose the chains of injustice and untie the cords of the yoke, to set the oppressed free and break every yoke? Is it not to **share your food with the hungry and to provide the poor wanderer with shelter — when you see the naked, to clothe him, and not to turn away from your own flesh and blood?** Then your light will break forth like the dawn, and your healing will quickly appear; then your righteousness will go before you, and the glory of the Lord will be your rear guard. Then you will call, and the Lord will answer; you will cry for help, and he will say: Here am I. If you do away with the yoke of oppression, with the pointing finger and malicious talk, and if you spend yourselves in behalf of the hungry and satisfy the needs of the*

oppressed, then your light will rise in the darkness, and your night will become like the noonday." (Isaiah 58:1-10)

GOD'S ANGER AND RESULTING DISCIPLINE WILL CREATE MULTIPLE CLASSES OF POOR:

"After you have had children and grandchildren and have lived in the land a long time — if you then become corrupt and make any kind of idol, doing evil in the eyes of the Lord your God and provoking him to anger, I call heaven and earth as witnesses against you this day that you will quickly perish from the land that you are crossing the Jordan to possess. You will not live there long but will certainly be destroyed. The Lord will scatter you among the peoples, and only a few of you will survive among the nations to which the Lord will drive you. There you will worship man-made gods of wood and stone, which cannot see or hear or eat or smell. But if from there you seek the Lord your God, you will find him if you look for him with all your heart and with all your soul. When you are in distress and all these things have happened to you, then in later days you will return to the Lord your God and obey him. For the Lord your God is a merciful God; he will not abandon or destroy you or forget the covenant with your forefathers, which he confirmed to them by oath." (Deuteronomy 4:25-31)

In this passage, we see how God loved Israel and entrusted them with much: To be caretakers of His Word and to bear the Messiah. Yet God warned: *"If you then become corrupt...doing evil in the eyes of the Lord your God,"* then *"the Lord will scatter you among the peoples, and only a few of you will survive among the nations to which the Lord will drive you."* The same applies to any nation God entrusts with much yet becomes corrupted.

Now that nation is America.

THOSE WITH MUCH MUST CARE FOR THE POOR

"From everyone who has been given much, much will be demanded; and from the one who has been entrusted with much, much more will be asked." (Luke 12:48)

God blessed America and Americans. He also gave Americans the responsibility of caring for the poor. When Jesus said, *"The poor you will always have with you, but you will not always have me,"* (Mt. 26:11) He was not giving us an out. Some think, Well, since we'll always have the poor, and there's nothing we can do, then we need not do anything. **No!** The Lord is telling us we'll always have the poor to serve, and **by serving them, we serve Him**.

All throughout history, the rich and powerful have taken advantage of the poor. God will judge them by how they handled the poor. The poor are also a test for Christians to see if we love Jesus. I'm not implying anyone must take care of all of the poor. But to pass God's test, we should have Jesus' compassion to take care of "our" poor, the poor that God planned for you to care for. We cannot take care of all the homeless but we may have compassion to prevent one of our loved ones from becoming homeless or otherwise joining the ranks of those in poverty.

"When you reap the harvest of your land, do not reap to the very edges of your field or gather the gleanings of your harvest. Leave them for the poor and the alien. I am the Lord your God." (Leviticus 23:22)

Those entrusted with fields and a large harvest were to help the poor by leaving some for them. Even that little can mean a lot to one of the poor. Even your one act can mean the world to one. Or, as Mother Theresa said, **"Everyone can do something."**

AMERICAN PHARISEES

"Jesus entered the temple area and drove out all who were buying and selling there. He overturned the tables of the money changers and the benches of those selling doves. 'It is written,' he said to them, "'My house will be called a house of prayer,'" but you are making it a "den of robbers."'" (Matthew 21:12-13)

The religious leaders and businessmen of the city were robbing the people. Whereas God desires leaders to care for citizens, these had set up a system to defraud the people. The Pharisees were the religious leaders in power and the businessmen were their allies. Together they got rich off the poor.

America is in a similar situation today. The rich control the government via elections, bureaucratic selections, and by setting-up laws that benefit themselves. Meanwhile, church leaders have stood by watching. We may not be as bad as the Pharisees, but we're bad enough! **We have not pointed out the way Christians should go as related to politics for fear of jeopardizing our 501 C(3) non-profit status.**

Further, we've systematically dismantled the Constitution in our ignorance, lackadaisical attitude, and by sins of omission. We have not recognized God's Hand. And worse, we've put money before God. How? By not wanting to rattle the businesspeople in our churches who donate a lot. Any tax risk might be unacceptable to them. The clincher? **We simply don't want the hassle of hordes of people complaining that church and politics don't mix.**

Of course, our churches justify what we're doing by our good works. *But is losing incremental amounts of our religious freedom each year worth it? Are we pleasing Jesus?* (Keep in mind, I include myself in this group. I'm the worst of all as both a businessman and pastor!)

Meanwhile, the poor suffer under the "fools" in government. Because of their policies, a whole segment of our middle class is sinking slowly and surely into poverty. At the present rate, I would not be surprised to see 50% of our middle class living in poverty within 10-15 years.

GOD'S THOUGHTS FOR US: IS GOD USING THE POOR TO HUMBLE US?

"Your attitude should be the same as that of Christ Jesus: Who, being in very nature God, did not consider equality with God something to be grasped, but made himself nothing, taking the very nature of a servant, being made in human likeness. And being found in appearance as a man, he humbled himself and became obedient to death — even death on a cross!" (Philippians 2:5-8)

God turned my heart to the poor by calling Diana and me into our ministry at Cedar Assembly of God. It wasn't just about doing ministry, God had another plan.

We had been involved in the ministry for over two years at Hawaii Cedar Church when one of our members Charley M. ended up in the hospital. Diana suggested that I go and visit Charley but my schedule was tight and I missed it. The next day the Holy Spirit prompted me. (Diana had given me that "look" the night before when I told her I had not gone.) She and I went together.

Charley looked bad. He wasn't conscious (although he may have been aware we were there). We prayed for him and left. The next day we received word that God had taken Charley.

That night, Diana told me: "Eh, you better get serious about this church thing."

I asked her, "Well, are you all in?"

She replied, "I guess so."

I said, "Now's the time to decide. We won't go forward if you don't think this is what God is doing."

She thought for a few seconds and finally said, "No, I'm in."

Charley's funeral was on December 12, 2009. It was my first time officiating a funeral. The place was packed with unfamiliar faces. We were late, thanks to traffic and a jammed schedule; and though I had a prepared message, I hadn't thought about an opening prayer. So when I opened, my first words were: "Father, bless this food that we're about to have...." *Oh, shoots!*

There was no recovering so I just kept going. It came out fine. I knew Charley well enough, God was lifted up, and I preached on heaven and Jesus coming back to take us (John 14).

There's nothing like a booboo to keep us humble. Thank God for old age because most of my booboo memory is wiped out. God's giant wand of grace can erase. But the thing is I couldn't help thinking about my booboo all that night and into the following week. Funny, I knew there was nothing I could do about it, but the video playback still ran in my mind.

I thought, *Well, maybe they thought I was blessing the food early.* Then I wondered, *What could I have said to recover?* The best idea: "Bless this food that we're about to have, **the food of Your Word!**" *Why wasn't I sharp enough to recover!* So much time wasted in meaningless thoughts.

The point is that over my life, I've spent thousands of hours on mental exercises to protect my self-image. Honestly, no one at the funeral probably even cared. But I wouldn't let it go. All those useless mind games and the needless stress on my physical and mental state over the years.

GOD WANTS THE BEST FOR US & THE BEST ATTITUDE? HUMILITY

"To fear the Lord is to hate evil; I hate pride and arrogance, evil behavior and perverse speech." (Proverbs 8:13)

C.S. Lewis wrote:

> "According to Christian teachers, the essential vice, the utmost evil, is Pride. Unchastity, anger, greed, drunkenness, and all that, are mere fleabites in comparison: it was through Pride that the devil became the devil: Pride leads to every other vice: it is the complete anti-God state of mind.
>
> "Does this seem to you exaggerated? If so, think it over. I pointed out a moment ago that the more pride one had, the more one disliked pride in others. In fact, if you want to find out how proud you are the easiest way is to ask yourself, 'How much do I dislike it when other people snub me, or refuse to take any notice of me, or shove their oar in, or patronise me, or show off?' …Greed may drive men into competition if there is not enough to go round; but the proud man, even when he has got more than he can possibly want, will try to get still more just to assert his power. Nearly all those evil in the world which people put down to greed or selfishness are really far more the result of Pride.
>
> "…The Christians are right: it is Pride which has been the chief cause of misery in every nation and every family since the world began." (C.S. Lewis, Mere Christianity, p. 121-123, Harper Collins e-books, 1952, 1980, N.Y.)

C.S. Lewis presents the compelling case that **pride is the greatest sin**. Not greed, sex, or addiction. This means I'm the worst of all sinners, alongside Apostle Paul. And it may explain why God loves the poor so much: The poor are not very prideful. They have nothing to be proud about. The have many sins, and many causes of their sins. Some use drugs and alcohol, and steal to support their habit. They end up homeless and have difficulty finding their way back.

Many who come through our church will end up dying on the street. My assistant pastor Darrick shared a thought once: "When they get saved, then what? They cannot get a job. They cannot find a place to live. They go back to their tents." Yet they come back to church every week. At least it's a place where they know someone loves them. And they know His Name.

The poor are not perfect in the humility department. They don't have much, but most will protect what little they do have. If someone presses their button, they're quick to react.

TSUKIJI MARKET PROGRAM

We have a discipleship group that is a part of our membership, core leaders, and servers in our church. The group consists of about 40 strong and some have been with us since our inception, March 25, 2007. Many have been with us for 3-4 years, and the rest 1-3 years. Since we have service and programs on Sundays, Tuesdays, Wednesdays, and every other Friday, there's a lot of work. We serve a simple breakfast and lunch when we're there.

When we have that many interacting, serving, and ministering to the poor, sparks will fly. We all do our best to react to tension with love, but we all have automatic horns in our chests that sound off at the slightest slight. So we've tried all kinds of resolution programs. Our current program is the "Tsukiji Market Program": If we can go three full weeks with no one's "horns blasting," then Cedar AOG will take the whole crew out for a celebration meal at Tsukiji Market (sushi buffet). Each week stands on its own, we're not looking for three consecutive weeks. Also, we all go, or no one goes. No one is left behind.

As I write this, we are about three months into our program and so far we have one week with a perfect score. It's obvious that pride is at the root of failure. However, the good news is we've incorporated failure into our program. Rather than implementing a strict legalistic disciplinary program, we recognize what Pastor Darrick says: **"We are built to fail; but we are not failures."** Paul confirms: *"For God has bound all men over to disobedience so that he may have mercy on them all"* (Rom. 11:32).

Our focus is on making the failure right. So when they fail, we don't want them to stomp off in anger and never come back. We hope our church is the most loving, cool (we have air conditioning), fun (game days), enjoyable (movie days) place with the best food in town. That way they have to come back or they miss out. When they come back, 95% go up to the person that initiated or recieved the blow up, and say the magic word: "Sorry," and shake hands. I can see God working out good and humility in His people.

PRIDE & ARROGANCE

As I understand Proverbs 8:13: *"To fear the LORD is to hate evil; I hate pride and arrogance..."* and reconcile it with C.S. Lewis, here's my thought: **Pride** is an **inward feeling** in our heart where we think that because of gifts, talents, accomplishments, money, power or prestige, we are better than others. Paul says our attitude should be that of Christ Jesus. Therefore, pride is an attitude toward life.

Arrogance is the **outward expression** of pride in putting down the next person: "I am better than you: I have more money. I am smarter. I am more powerful. I am more famous. I can break you."

God hates both pride and arrogance.

These twisted twins have haunted me all of my life. Early on, I was not very smart, talented, strong, or quick-witted (Lloyd Fujie in our

"Safaris" gang was the undisputed king of wits). I was always a "wan-nabe." So my pride rating (0 = Jesus, 100 = Satan when he fell) may have been on the lower end.

Diana was a gem; it didn't matter to her that I wasn't the great-est. She loved me as I was, and I always felt special to her. I never remember her "talking smack" or even saying the smallest negative. Whenever we were in groups, like with a contractor at a business din-ner, the wives would eventually get engrossed in their conversation. But my ears have a special tuning fork that can hear whenever Diana might be giving me praise. My heart would *hum* during those times!

One thing I always remember was coming home to share a big victory, a big job, a smart move, or a shrewd deal with Diana. It real-ly wasn't the sharing of celebration that quickened my heart; I was boasting about how great I was. Diana's favorite actor has always been Sean Connery (even before "007"). So I took the name "007": after all, my first name is James!

As "007," I boasted about my deals. Diana was always a polite lis-tener. God was orchestrating good: He knew I needed my wife behind me all the way, so He prepared her to be a "007" leading lady.

As God brought success to A-1, my pride rating increased; I thought I was brilliant. I became a Vice President. Even after almost crashing and burning the business twice (1976-1985), the success in the late 80s made me smug. I had arrived! I had survived the tough times; now I had it all. It also changed my relationship with Diana. Now I was the real deal "007." My head got bigger (so my hair fell out).

I thank God that He didn't give up on me, but drew me to Christ in early 1993. Then I was exposed to truth and He began to change my pride rating. It leveled off for a season. He had let me have it "my way" for 45 years, but He had a plan.

So my first three to four years as a Christian, I resolved to love Diana as God loved me. I would not ask "why" questions and tried my best not to react by blasting my "horn." Diana eventually recognized that her samurai had no sword, so she took out her knife.

God was working "good" for Diana and for me. A song by a group called Passenger sings, *"Only know you love her when you let her go."* This reflects what God has been doing, especially these last 10 years of our marriage. Once I let Diana go to develop on her own, God did what only He could in ministry. It allowed Him to raise her up.

Today God is using Diana in a huge way at our church. I think the people love her more than they love me, but since we're one, I count that towards my account. Of course, Diana is on one of our cooking crews and our people love food. No one remembers what I preached last week but they remember her shoyu chicken. And they remember her banana cream pie or apple cobbler with ice cream. Good thing we're together as one!

Recently Diana got really angry at me. I made a statement and she said, "That's why I hate talking to you!" She got up, threw her dishes in the sink (she wasn't finished with breakfast), and stormed off. I had been sleeping at my mom's house to help her, so I didn't see my wife for two nights. When I came home, first thing, I said, "I'm sorry, I'm wrong. I love you and wouldn't want to do anything to hurt you."

During the two days while I was away, I realized that when I was at a pastor meeting the week before, my prayer included asking God to humble me and help me with pride. Of course, I didn't really think I needed help, but it sounds good in a prayer. But God knew I needed it. Be careful what you pray, He *always* answers prayer.

IF GOD ACCOMPLISHES EVERYTHING, WHAT ROOM IS THERE FOR PRIDE?

Pride has two footholds in our souls: First, we all have a "base pride" even if we haven't accomplished anything great. Second is a "personal pride" that grows with accomplishment. For the sake of illustration,

I'll establish an arbitrary rating system: (Remember: 0 = Jesus, 100 = Satan when he fell.)

PRIDE RATING CHART: (My Arbitrary Rating)

	Pride Rating
Person with no accomplishments	30
Person with some accomplishments	40-50
Person with great accomplishments	60-80
Person on top of the world	90-95
Person beaten down by the world	20-30

As I look back, the Scripture that helped me most in balancing accomplishment with *"putting to death my pride"* was from Isaiah: *"Lord...all that we have accomplished you have done for us"* (Isa. 26:12). All the good at A-1 was not by my doing, but by God's Hand.

Where I thought I was smooth and shrewd, it was God giving favor with general contractors. Where I thought I had set-up our job costing, change order, and project management systems, God's Hand was there. I thought I was a marketing genius (shame to say) to major general contractors and selling them on using A-1. I presented our firm as a large firm with massive engineering, project engineering and management capacity; we were woefully lacking. But I was being shrewd like a "007."

However, God was working on dropping my pride rating. Once I recognized that I should not be proud of the very thing that gave me a boost, our company, I was humbled. It moved my pride rating of 80 back to 40. It did not completely diminish my "base pride." God did not look from heaven and think all was well with this guy who still thought he could be "007."

LIVING LIFE WITH FAMILY SEALS THE DEAL

The key is not just understanding Scripture, but actually living it out. Impossible, sure, but Jesus said we should shoot for perfection. I imagine God speaking to me personally and telling me (like my mother used to): "Jimmy Boy, all you think you accomplished, I did for you."

The Lord had a lot of work left in helping me to become more humble. I may never get to a 10 (A-) or 20 (B-) rating, but God's still working! And once I recognize that **everything God gave us was for eternal impact** — my gifts and talents, our business (A-1 A-lectrician), my ministry — then I've got it right. It's ALL for His glory, not my pride.

It dawned upon me that God knit Diana together and molded her over the years through her family. God knew I could not reach 67 years old without Diana. God used her to help bring my pride rating down, slowly.

LESSONS FROM MY CHILDREN

Jason, our oldest, was molded by God and has taken the reins of A-1. God orchestrated our securing of the Hawaii Regional Security Operations Center project, which God used to develop Jason in huge ways. At this stage, Jason is way ahead of where I was at 50 years of age. My dad ("Senior") started the business and Jason continues as the third generation. The best thing about Jason is that he loves God, sees His Hand at work, and trusts Him. Jason also grows in humility as he too believes what Isaiah wrote: *"Lord… all we have accomplished, you have done for us."*

When Jason graduated from the University of Hawaii with his business degree, he came to work at A-1. He was an electrician and worked in the field on the Tapa Tower Ballroom renovation. One night at the dinner table, Jason shared about a foreman being too harsh on him. What Jason didn't realize was all of the foremen knew they were developing the next leader of the company. They treated him like any other electrician and may have hurt his feelings (poor thing).

So he ranted on and my volcano went off: "Jason, ***###***!!!"
(It wasn't pretty but at least no "F" word.) There were other ways of
speaking truth with agape, but I couldn't bear him even *seeming* disrespectful. Jason was seeking fairness, but his dad wouldn't listen. I've
since apologized many times.

You see, the job didn't hang on our discussion, it was my pride.
God was working on me.

Daven, our second son, moved to Vallejo ('Frisco Bay area) with
his wife Charity and daughter Madi. He also recognizes that God is
involved in everything he accomplishes. He has seen God do marvel-
ous and miraculous things and I've seen God use Daven.

God has also used Daven to work on me. Last year on a trip to
Disneyland, we were in Oakland waiting for a flight to LAX. We were
eating and my son had something to share: He said I didn't listen to
him completely, like I was always trying to correct him. He hoped I
would listen better. I agreed to try, but I thought I already did.
Why is it that when those you love most share a simple cry, we still
don't do well? Soon after, I realized God was still working on my
humility. He never stops.

My favorite (and only) daughter **Lisa** grew up remembering Dad as
"super strict." Until she was eight years old. Once I came to know
Jesus that changed. I tried to be a gentler, kinder dad who lived grace.
As time went by, Lisa gained more and more freedom in being who
God wanted her to be. The quiet, respectful little daddy's girl who
lived in fear of "The DAD" was allowed to express her feelings, which
were repressed while she was younger.

One day, when Lisa was around 12 or 13, I corrected her about
a small thing. She hadn't put something away and I called her to the
living room and asked her nicely to do so. She stomped into the room,
picked up the item, and stomped off in a huff. Disrespectful.

In living life with my family, I realize that God is working things out for good in their lives, and growing each of them to be the person He wants them to be. One of my early foundation Scriptures for living was, "...*continue to work out your salvation with fear and trembling, for it is God who works in you to will and to act according to his good purpose*" (Philip. 2:12-13). Many more Scriptures teach that God will work in Lisa, Daven, Jason, and Diana to be the person He wants them to be. I simply need to get out of the way.

But it's not just about God working in them, it's also about God working in me. He wants me to become like His Son; to grow in humility, the antithesis of pride. God gives principles for my family so that as I apply these truths, He can work humility in me. God uses my kids and wife to grow my humility.

IF GREATEST SIN IS PRIDE, & AMERICA IS PRIDEFUL, THEN GOD WILL HUMBLE AMERICA

Any Bible study of the Middle East clearly shows God disciplines and humbles all nations, including Egypt, Assyria, Babylon, Israel and many more. To do so God always uses divine measures: loss of economic wealth and the loss of production, disease and sickness, insect invasion (locust, etc.), other nations invading and ravaging, and ultimate humbling of the target nation. In many cases, God declared that those nations would never rise again as a ruling power.

America is headed down the same path. **His humbling will return America's greatness**.

In the next chapter, we'll look at what God desires of us. He will give us our mission as we approach the Last Days.

CHAPTER 5

WHAT IS GOD DOING?

*"And we know that God causes everything to work
together for the good of those who love God and are called
according to his purpose for them.
For God knew his people in advance, and he chose
them to become like his Son...."*
(Romans 8:28-29, NLT)

ARE WE IN THE LAST DAYS?
IF SO, APPROXIMATELY WHERE ARE WE?

Only a foolish person would try to think what God is doing in the world today, yet I must try! (I also must differentiate a foolish person from a "fool": one who doesn't think God exists or doesn't think God wants anything to do with us.) I am foolish because I love God but I'll try to use all the "God Logic" I can muster with my 5%-usage brain to answer the question, **"What is God Doing?"**

The task begins with a good reference point. Then we may work our way backwards, look at possibilities, and guess the most probable scenario. And that's how we will find our answer.

Our reference point: Revelation 21, the end of the Bible — Victory in Christ Jesus!

> *"Then I saw a new heaven and a new earth, for the first heaven and the first earth had passed away, and there was no longer any sea. I saw the Holy City, the New Jerusalem, coming down out of heaven from God, prepared as a bride beautifully dressed for her husband. And I heard a loud voice from the throne saying, 'Now the dwelling of God is with men, and he will live with them. They will be his people, and God himself will be with them and be their God. He will wipe every tear from their eyes. There will be no more death or mourning or crying or pain, for the old order of things has passed away.'"* (Revelation 21:1-4)

In the end, **WE WIN!** Our ultimate end point (Rev. 21) is also our "starting point." From this Eternal Victory, we work our way back to our present. So, prior to that (Rev. 20), Satan is thrown into the lake of fire along with those who are not born again, those whose names are not written in the Book of Life.

Prior to that was the fall of Babylon, the great trading city destroyed (Rev. 18). What might this great city look like today? Here are some clues (characteristics) of "Babylon":

1. (vs. 2) *"She has become a home for demons and a haunt for every evil spirit, a haunt for every unclean and detestable bird."*
2. (vs. 3) *"Kings (nations) committed adultery with her, and merchants (traders)... grew rich from her excessive luxuries."*
3. (vs. 4) She received plagues from God because of her many sins.
4. (vs. 7) She was proud and arrogant, lived in luxury and boasted, *"I sit as queen; I am not a widow, and I will never mourn."*
5. (vs. 9) The nations that *"committed adultery"* with the city, *"will weep and mourn over her"* when they see the *"smoke of her burning."* In other words, it will happen quickly.

6. (vs. 10) *"In **one hour** your doom has come!"* In God's time, one hour could be one hour, one day, or 40 years.
7. (vs. 11-13) The merchant (nations) traded every type of precious cargo.
8. (vs. 14-17) The merchant (nations) became wealthy from trading with her.
9. (vs. 18) This is the greatest city or nation, if symbolic.
10. (vs. 23-24) *"Your merchants were the world's great men. By your magic spell all the nations were led astray. In her was found the blood of prophets and of the saints, and of all who have been killed on the earth."*

Bible commentaries differ on exactly who is Babylon, though they seem to agree on these possibilities:

    * **The Latin Church** (Adam Clarke, Commentary & Critical Notes, Adam Clarke's Commentary, Electronic Database. 2006 by Biblesoft, Inc.)

    * **Papal Rome** (Albert Barnes, 1798-1870, from Barnes' Notes, Electronic Database 2006 by Biblesoft, Inc.)

    * **City of Rome** (Gill)

    * **The great commercial center of the world**
(J. Vernon McGee)

Regardless of who the city represents, we know that she encourages evil everywhere and others grow rich off her excessive luxury. She's proud and arrogant and receives many plagues. Her partner nations in trade become rich and her merchants are the world's great men. The city itself is the greatest ever. Ultimately, wickedness and the demonic will rule, and plagues will impact the multitudes.

We see this evident in the world today as the top 1% (super-rich) own almost 50% of the world's wealth. A study by USA Today confirms this unfortunate truth: "Further, this poorer 'bottom half' now has about the same amount of money as the richest 85 people in the world, and the wealthiest grew their share of bounty in 24 out of 26 countries surveyed between 1980 and 2012." (USA Today, Kevin A. Kepple, Jeff Dionise & Anne R. Carey; January 20, 2014)

This means the super-rich grew their wealth on the backs of the poor in their nations.

However, Revelation 18 shows that this all will fall.

Continuing our quest for "What is God Doing," we take a quantum leap, before Babylon's fall, is the Second Coming of Jesus and the Rapture. (Remember, we're moving backward in time to our present.)

Prior to the Rapture of the saints, we find ourselves living in the Last Days.

BIBLICAL TEACHINGS ON THE LAST DAYS

The Bible sounds an alarm to warn us that we are in the Last Days. Here's a detailed list to watch for:

"In the last days, God says, I will pour out my Spirit on all people" (Acts 2:17).

This happened 10 days after Jesus' ascent into heaven. The Spirit came upon many. And He lives in all of us who accept Christ as Lord. Here are more Last Days details to be alert for:

"There will be terrible times in the last days. People will be lovers of themselves, lovers of money, boastful, proud, abusive, disobedient to their parents, ungrateful, unholy, without love, unforgiving, slanderous, without self-control, brutal, not lovers of the good, treacherous, rash, conceited, lovers of pleasure rather than lovers of God—having a form of godliness but denying its power. Have nothing to do with them." (2 Timothy 3:1-5)

"Now listen, you rich people, weep and wail because of the misery that is coming upon you. Your wealth has rotted, and moths have

*eaten your clothes. Your gold and silver are corroded. Their corrosion will testify against you and eat your flesh like fire. You have **hoarded wealth** in the last days."* (James 5:1-3)

"Hoarded wealth" will not be useful possibly because no one will be producing anything in those days. The super-rich and powerful "fools" would do well to listen; or re-read Revelation 18, the fall of all.

JESUS' TEACHINGS ON THE LAST DAYS

The disciples asked Jesus, *"What will be the sign of you coming and of the end of the age?"* Jesus answered to watch out for these things: (Matthew 24)

vs. 6: *"Wars and rumors of wars...."*

vs. 7: *"Nation will rise up against nation, and kingdom against kingdom...*
"...famines and earthquakes in various places...."

vs. 9: Christians will be *"persecuted and put to death."*
and, *"...will be hated by all nations because of me."*

vs. 10: *"Many will turn away from the faith and betray and hate each other...."*

vs. 11: *"False prophets will appear and deceive many people."*

vs. 12: *"Because of the increase of wickedness, the love of most will grow cold."*

Jesus' dire list of disasters is further advance warning for us to keep in mind as we develop a picture of what the Last Days may look like. Are these events happening now? If so, what do we do? But, as the TV pitchman used to always say, **there's more...**

"GREAT DISTRESS"

*"Then there will be **great distress**, unequaled from the beginning of the world until now—and never to be equaled again. If those days*

had not been cut short, no one would survive, but for the sake of the elect those days will be shortened." (Matthew 24:21-23)

*"How dreadful it will be in those days for pregnant women and nursing mothers! There will be **great distress** in the land and wrath against this people." (Luke 21:23-24)*

The Last Days cover a large period of time from Jesus' day until His return. Is that now? Let's recap some of the common themes through the Scriptures, Last Days through Revelation 18:

* Scoffers will scoff: *"There is no God."*

* The rich will get richer and richer.

* People will love themselves, money; be boastful, disobedient to their parents; love pleasure and become seekers of godliness, but not God; and follow their own evil desires.

- Evil and wickedness will reign as people follow their own evil desires in cities and nations.
- Christians will be hated (by all nations), persecuted and put to death.
- There will be wars (nation against nation), famines, and earthquakes (and resulting tsunamis).
- Christians will turn away from their faith, betray and hate each other.
- But the worst of all: Agape love of Christians (for only they have Agape) will grow cold.

The spookiest passage is where Jesus warns of *"great distress, unequaled from the beginning of the world until now — and never to be equaled again."* This means that whatever evil we see now is about to get much worse. **We are living in the Last Days**, and are headed into times of *"great distress."*

The Old Testament saw gruesome times: starvation, plagues, mass executions, eating babies, infant sacrifices to gods, crucifixions, beheadings, burning people alive, people sacrificed to be eaten by wild animals, rapes, murders, mass marches under brutal conditions, and more. Yet Jesus warns that **what is yet to come will be the absolute worst!**

This *"great distress,"* is yet ahead of us. We don't know if it is 10, 50, or 100 years out, but we do know it's coming. We also know that wars and rumors of wars, earthquakes, famines, and persecution of Christians are already taking place. Which means soon a great mess will unfold.

God is orchestrating events (Is. 46:10) by allowing Satan and evil to run rampant. He does so by allowing Satan more freedom with evil men who do not believe and therefore have no restraint (Job 1-2, 1 Chron. 21:1, 2 Sam. 24:1). It can be difficult to see God working good from the unfolding events. God is surely teaching us His sovereignty and we must walk by faith, not by what we *think* we see ahead.

FOCUS: GOD IS WORKING FOR THE GOOD OF THE WORLD

Remember, God is causing all things to work together for everyone's good (Rom. 8:28) because He loves the nations, the world, even the unbelieving sinner. There was never a time that God didn't have each one of us on His mind. Jesus is sitting at the right hand of the Father, interceding for us ceaselessly! Yet God also **disciplines** those He loves out of a heart that wants them to respond to Him (Heb. 12). And although God may seem unfair, unkind, or unjust, keep in mind what He said through King David:

> *"For I envied the arrogant when I saw the prosperity of the wicked. They have no struggles; their bodies are healthy and strong. They are free from the burdens common to man; they are not plagued by human ills. Therefore pride is their necklace; they clothe themselves*

with violence. From their callous hearts comes iniquity; the evil conceits of their minds know no limits. They scoff, and speak with malice; in their arrogance they threaten oppression. Their mouths lay claim to heaven, and their tongues take possession of the earth. Therefore their people turn to them and drink up waters in abundance. They say, 'How can God know? Does the Most High have knowledge?' This is what the wicked are like — always carefree, they increase in wealth. Surely in vain have I kept my heart pure; in vain have I washed my hands in innocence. All day long I have been plagued; I have been punished every morning. If I had said, 'I will speak thus,' "I would have betrayed your children. When I tried to understand all this, it was oppressive to me till I entered the sanctuary of God; then I understood their final destiny."'" (Psalm 73:3-17)

Unless we recognize and truly believe that eternity with Christ is the only thing that will count in this world, the future doesn't make sense. All of the devastation and destruction, the evil and wickedness, the hunger and trials, the hurt and the pain that millions will endure (even us and our loved ones) seems too much to bear. It will be impossible to stand strong save for Christ.

MISERY IS GOOD TONIC

God's main desire is that people come to know Him through His Son, Jesus, and then become like Him. For those who are "fools" (don't believe in Jesus), God has a Master plan: He allows them to get to a point of misery that will cause them to dig deep down into their souls and look up to Him. God puts within us things that will draw us to Him. Once we lose everything, we realize we have no other hope:

"For I will be like a lion to Ephraim, like a great lion to Judah. I will tear them to pieces and go away; I will carry them off, with no one to rescue them. Then I will go back to my place until they admit

*their guilt. And they will seek my face; **in their misery they will earnestly seek me**.*" (Hosea 5:14-15)

The super-rich have a disadvantage: They have unlimited resources so they have a harder time hitting a point of misery. Death is their last opportunity, so God uses death. Everyone dies. Even the super-rich.

Those that are poor hit their "misery threshold" quickly; they're more apt to look up, cry out, and hang on to God as they undergo God's lion attack. They seek His face and quickly embrace the Gospel of Jesus Christ. Even so, they need more than salvation; sanctification requires the Word become alive for them, or they don't have true living transformation.

AMERICA TODAY: FULFILLS THE BIBLICAL MODEL OF THE LAST DAYS

What's happening in America today lines up with the Bible's detailed description of the Last Days. We may argue that some nations are worse off. But they may argue that we're the worst!

Benjamin Disraeli, the 19th century British Prime Minister, once said: "There are three kinds of lies: lies, damned lies, and statistics." I could bore you with more statistics about America's demise but I've already done that in earlier chapters (see Ch. 3 & 4). Plus, I don't want any "fools" calling me a liar.

WORLD TODAY: ALSO FULFILLS BIBLICAL MODEL OF LAST DAYS

The Tower of Babel gives us a glimpse of God's heart: The whole world had developed one language, a common speech. Their unity caused a pride that swelled up in a perverted plan, a shared goal of building a tower *"that reaches to the heavens, so that we may make a name for ourselves and not be scattered over the face of the whole earth"* (Gen. 11:4).

The Lord was not pleased and *"confuse[d] the people with different languages. Then they won't be able to understand each other"* (Gen. 11:7, NLT). When He did that, they scattered across the earth.

When I first became a Christian, I used to wake up to J. Vernon McGee. He had a raspy ole voice that was quite unusual and rather difficult to listen to. But at 5 a.m., it was a good wake-up call. He believed in the power of the Word of God and aimed to preach through the entire Bible. He did so in five years. I loved it, he would read the Word, give commentary, and always share stories to bring life to the Word. Some Bible scholars may take him to be a "kook" for his free-spirited opinions meshed with the Word of God. As a pastor, I can look back now and say that I really liked J. Vernon McGee's style. Maybe because all my life, as a man who (wrongly) thought he knew everything, and freely offered his opinions to all who would listen, I connected. He has an interesting message on the destruction of Babel:

> "Let me ask you a question: Was this a blessing in disguise, or was it a curse upon mankind? Well, for God's purposes it was a blessing. For man's development away from God, it was definitely a judgment. Down through the centuries mankind has been kept separate, and it has been a great hindrance to him. One thing that is happening today through the medium of radio and television and jet travel is that these walls are being broken down. They are tumbling down like the walls of Jericho. This is one reason that I believe God is coming down in judgment again." (p. 97, Tower of Babel Revisited, "Through the Bible," J. Vernon McGee, Thomas Nelson Publishers, Nashville, TN)

J. Vernon McGee would be in utter shock at the state of the world today. He wrote his commentary in the late 70s when the Internet, iPhones and iPads, tweets and texts, all social media were non-existent. Let's take a closer look at the whole passage to see his point:

"The Lord said, 'If as one people speaking the same language they have begun to do this, then nothing they plan to do will be impossible for them. Come, let us go down and confuse their language so they will not understand each other.' So the Lord scattered them from there over all the earth, and they stopped building the city. That is why it was called Babel — because there the Lord confused the language of the whole world. From there the Lord scattered them over the face of the whole earth." (Genesis 11:5-9)

God purposely separated the people via different languages so they wouldn't become too great and powerful in their own eyes. Today the super-rich cross language barriers to speak one common language: money. The American dollar is the world's currency. The super-rich "talk" to each other no matter if they are American, German, French, Chinese, Indian, Russian, Arab, Brazilian, or Japanese.

If God were to break down the "common language" of today's modern Babel, He would only have to break the almighty dollar from its lofty position to split the world again. When that happens (and I believe it is soon), many nations will fight for their currency to replace the dollar as the world currency. None will succeed; God will see to that.

IF JESUS IS COMING SOON, WE SHOULD
SEE EXTREMELY TOUGH TIMES TODAY

The Bible is clear: One day Jesus will return in judgment. We don't know when that is, but looking around, we can already see the evil and wickedness that the Bible predicts prior to His return. That means He's coming soon. When I first became a Christian, I used to hear pastors preach and teach on the return of Jesus Christ using Matthew 24. That's where Jesus alerted us on what to watch for:

"You will hear of wars and rumors of wars, but see to it that you are not alarmed. Such things must happen, but the end is still to come. Nation will rise against nation, and kingdom against kingdom. There will be famines and earthquakes in various places. All these are the beginning of birth pains. Then you will be handed over to be persecuted and put to death, and you will be hated by all nations because of me. At that time many will turn away from the faith and will betray and hate each other, and many false prophets will appear and deceive many people. Because of the increase of wickedness, the love of most will grow cold, but he who stands firm to the end will be saved. And this gospel of the kingdom will be preached in the whole world as a testimony to all nations, and then the end will come." (Matthew 24:6-14)

Many preachers on this topic teach on the increase of wars, famines, and earthquakes. Some back it up with statistics, thinking the more statistics, the stronger the case, the more imminent His return. However, a simple reading does not require any increase. They simply need to exist:

- Wars
- Rumors of wars
- Famines
- Earthquakes in various places
- Christians persecuted to death
- Christians hated because of Jesus
- Christians turning away from their faith
- Christians betraying each other
- False prophets
- Increasing wickedness

All of these exist in the world today. The remaining (unsolvable) argument: Those who demand statistics don't agree on a common reference point. It would be impossible. A common reference point depends on a shared paradigm. Liberals and conservatives have nothing in common in this area. So they always end up using their own sets of statistics. **Therefore, the fact that all of these predicted conditions exist is enough to validate that we live within the Day of His return. We're in the Last Days.**

AGAPE LOVE GROWING COLD

The most telltale warning from Jesus to confirm we're in the Last Days: *"Because of the increase of wickedness, the love of most will grow cold..."* (Mt. 24:12). There's no doubt of the increase in wickedness. Statistics are not needed, for if you do not already see it, statistics will not help you see.

What we don't know is whether each of the wicked situations would be 30%, 60%, 90% or 99% fulfilled for His imminent return (read: next year). What we also don't know is if God requires each condition to reach 100% for His return. Also, we don't know how each wicked condition will accelerate so that even though it took 2,000 years since Jesus rose from the dead to get to a certain percentage, the quantum acceleration in wickedness may be such that Jesus returns next year.

I am not predicting the time of His return, but I am raising possibilities.

It's like the financial crash of 2008, caused by subprime loans. Many "in the know" saw it coming, but few were truly prepared when it hit. They believed their bank or financial firms were too big to fail and they could simply lobby government to "bail them out."

Some Christians (me included) are the same. We know Jesus will return one day, but we go on living as if nothing horrendous will happen prior to His return. We trust our faith is large enough so when the "Sh_t hits the fan," Jesus will just bail us out. Thank God for grace!

However, we're called to do more than just skinny through the fire alive.

GOD IS BUSTING & BANKRUPTING AMERICA, CREATING WHOLE NEW CLASSES OF POOR

Most recognize that America is busted and bankrupt, and we have a whole nation becoming poor. We have increasing homelessness, increasing number in poverty who require government assistance, an entire middle class is disintegrating, college graduates who will be disappointed they don't have expected opportunities, and the elderly with failing healthcare and falling incomes.

There is enough evidence in the Bible to conclude that God is orchestrating the fall of America. Including the systematic sinking of her economy, financial system, government, social order, and educational system. However, God will work out His ultimate good, by busting America.

Whether He is or not, the bigger issue is simple: **"How do we live?"**

What kind of attitude should we have going through this?

The ultimate objective is to become more like Jesus.

GOD'S GOOD FOR U.S. WILL PARALLEL GOD'S GOOD FOR US

I used to think that God was working for *my* good, first and foremost. Whatever was good for me must be good for those around me — my wife, business and family. Good was measured by fun, happiness, pleasure, worldly joy, and finances. Now I realize God the Father knows best. God's definition of a blessing is very different from what I define as a blessing. His blessings for America may look far different than what we may expect.

God wants people to know His Son, then become like His Son. He wants them to develop character. He desires that we live unconditional love, gentleness, kindness, godliness, choosing God's way rather than fulfilling our desires. Easier said than done! It's when we start actually living the life that it gets difficult. And remember, for some the years leading up to the day we received Jesus Christ as Lord and Savior were tough times.

Sanctification is a continuation of God working good. As people build character, they have to go through challenging times: "*Not only so, but we also* **rejoice in our sufferings**, *because we know that suffering produces perseverance; perseverance, character; and character, hope*" (Rom. 5:3-5).

As we go through the suffering, good comes from it: "*Hope does not disappoint us, because God has poured out his love into our hearts by the Holy Spirit, whom he has given us*" (Rom. 5:5). And what can be better than having the Agape love of Christ "*poured out into our hearts*"?

We must remember this is a lifelong process:

"*They devoted themselves to the apostles' teaching and to the fellowship, to the breaking of bread and to prayer. Everyone was filled with awe, and many wonders and miraculous signs were done by the apostles. All the believers were together and had everything in common. Selling their possessions and goods, they gave to anyone as he had need. Every day they continued to meet together in the temple courts. They broke bread in their homes and ate together with glad and sincere hearts, praising God and enjoying the favor of all the people. And the Lord added to their number daily those who were being saved.*" (Acts 2:42-47)

**If God is working out His ultimate plan for America,
what might that look like?**

"Experiencing God" author Henry Blackaby states: "Once I know what God is doing, then I see what I should do. My focus needs to be outward on God and His purposes, not inward on my life....But the plans He has for your life are based on what He is doing in the world around you. He has a larger purpose in mind for all humanity. His desire is for you to become involved in what He is doing to bring salvation to others. Discovering God's greater plan helps you know what He wants to do through you." (Experiencing God, Henry & Richard Blackaby and Claude King, 2008, B&H Publishing Group, Nashville, TN)

America is undergoing a tsunami. If I was in the ocean on a 22' Boston Whaler and a giant tsunami was coming, I wouldn't stay in front of the wave. I would do my best to get behind the wave and follow it in, then I'd be in good shape.

Our goal is to see His Hand working in America and follow Him. Whatever He's doing, I'm in!

WHAT IS GOD DOING IN AMERICA?

Keep in mind, we're maintaining a staunch belief that God is involved *intimately* in all things. I take this literally, but not for everything. Example: He didn't orchestrate what I ate for lunch and how much I ate.

Let's focus on the recent 50 years, specifically on what busted America:
1. God helped America win WWII; raising our nation as the world's leader—militarily, economically, socially, and educationally. The middle class grew in wealth and successive generations prospered.
2. Americans became prideful. Even the good kings in Israel who started off humble and loving God eventually allowed the greatest sin, pride, to infect their souls.
3. "Fools" (those who say there is no God) came into power and America turned her back on God, on the Constitution, and conse-

quently changed America's laws by judicial decree.

4. Americans then became disenchanted and disengaged from the political process and moved further from any responsibility in government.

5. God allowed America its freedom of choice (free will): Sin reigned as many "did their own thing," taking advantage of God's grace.

> "Furthermore, since they did not think it worthwhile to retain the knowledge of God, he gave them over to a depraved mind, to do what ought not to be done. They have become filled with every kind of wickedness, evil, greed and depravity. They are full of envy, murder, strife, deceit and malice. They are gossips, slanderers, God-haters, insolent, arrogant and boastful; they invent ways of doing evil; they disobey their parents; they are senseless, faithless, heartless, ruthless. Although they know God's righteous decree that those who do such things deserve death, they not only continue to do these very things but also approve of those who practice them." (Romans 1:28-32)

6. America became bankrupt and Americans became poor.

GOD IS MAKING AMERICANS POOR
SO HE CAN MAKE US RICH

> "Then the Spirit of God came upon Zechariah son of Jehoiada the priest. He stood before the people and said, 'This is what God says: "Why do you disobey the LORD's commands? You will not prosper. Because you have forsaken the LORD, he has forsaken you."'"
> (2 Chronicles 24:20)

> "Although the Aramean army had come with only a few men, the LORD delivered into their hands a much larger army. Because Judah had forsaken the LORD, the God of their fathers, judgment was executed on Joash." (2 Chronicles 24:24)

"Therefore, the LORD says: 'I am planning disaster against this people, from which you cannot save yourselves. You will no longer walk proudly, for it will be a time of calamity." (Micah 2:3)

Americans today (except for those in poverty) think they're the greatest nation on earth. They think it's their hard work, smarts, talent, and shrewdness that made America great. They forget it is God who made America great. And, to make it worse, they ignore His lessons on how to live.

AMERICA HAS FORGOTTEN GOD'S INSTRUCTIONS

America's foundation was built on the idea that its Creator blessed Americans with a country rich in resources and with freedom for all. God gave America responsibility to govern itself and help other nations. To do that, God gave our citizens the responsibility to elect our leaders. Why? He could not trust any one individual or group:

"It is better to take refuge in the Lord than to trust in man. It is better to take refuge in the Lord than to trust in princes." (Psalm 118:8-9)

*"Now while he was in Jerusalem at the Passover Feast, many people saw the miraculous signs he was doing and believed in his name. But **Jesus would not entrust himself to them, for he knew all men**. He did not need man's testimony about man, for he knew what was in a man."* (John 2:23-25)

God made a plan to keep our country on track by having the Founding Fathers set up a Constitution with three different branches, a checks-and-balances system against the sinful nature of man. That was abandoned long ago by the rich and powerful. Instead, they chose to enslave America by:

1. **Controlling elections**: They financially support candidates who pass laws favorable to them. To win, candidates need a large, organized machine and lots of money. Well-financed campaigns have a

huge advantage over starving ones.

2. **<u>Killing the will of the people by crushing hope and decimating participation</u>**: "Our elected officials don't listen to me so I won't vote."

3. **<u>Buying votes through social programs</u>** that appear to take care of the people. The people don't realize they're actually enabled and enslaved.

4. **<u>Taking financial advantage of man's sinful nature</u>**: lust of the eyes, cravings and pride. Movies, television, gambling, pornographic media, music, all cater to and profit on our sin nature.

5. **<u>Shipping jobs overseas</u>**: Business does this at the expense of caring for fellow Americans. Bottom line: Money before people.

BUSINE$$ & MONEY: FOUNDATION OF POLITIC$

As C.S. Lewis argued, our greatest sin is pride. America's pride has produced clear fruit: business, money, and politics. The brilliant Charles Krauthammer in his book "Things That Matter," says of politics:

> "...I left a life in medicine for a life in journalism devoted mostly to politics, while firmly believing that what really matters, what moves the spirit, what elevates the mind, what stirs the imagination, what makes us fully human are all of these endeavors, disciplines, confusions and amusements that lie outside politics.
>
> "Accordingly, this book was originally going to be a collection of my writings about everything but politics... Working title: 'There's More to Life than Politics.'
>
> "But in the end I couldn't. In the end (science, medicine, art, poetry, architecture, chess, space, sports, number theory) ... must bow to the sovereignty of politics.
>
> Politics...dominates everything because, in the end, everything—high and low...lives or dies by politics. You can have

the most advanced and efflorescent of cultures. Get your politics wrong, however, and everything stands to be swept away. This is not ancient history. This is Germany 1933." (Krauthammer, Charles; "Things That Matter: Three Decades of Passion, Pasttimes, & Politics," Crown Forum Publisher, 2013)

America has gotten its politics wrong (fools in power) and is now paying the price. Nothing works. All systems are broken. Any attempt to fix one has consequences in other areas and makes problems much worse. Fools then try another fix and things get worse again. **There is no end but THE END**.

Apostle Paul alerted us to the lifestyle, hearts and attitudes of people in power:

> "They will be lovers of themselves...money, boastful, proud, abusive...lovers of pleasure rather than lovers of God...." (2 Timothy 3:1-5)

> "They are the kind who worm their way into homes and gain control over weak-willed women, who are loaded down with sins and are swayed by all kinds of evil desires, always learning but never able to acknowledge the truth. Just as Jannes and Jambres opposed Moses, so also these men oppose the truth — men of depraved minds, who, as far as the faith is concerned, are rejected. But they will not get very far because, as in the case of those men, **their folly will be clear to everyone**." (2 Timothy 3:6-9)

Then Paul warned how these selfish "lovers" would gain control over the people:

1. By worming their way into homes: Today through media and enablement.
2. By gaining control over weak-willed people: The rich and powerful want the people uneducated, poor, homeless/ living in public

housing, on drugs and alcohol, living on subsidies, and fighting one another.

3. By loading people down with sin and tempting them with all kinds of evil desires: Money is their god and they do anything — lie, cheat, steal — to get it.

4. By making deals that influence every arena of our lives. These power brokers are intelligent and often college-educated; they write books or teach college classes. They rule the business, political, economic, and/or the financial and banking worlds. The make deals with the world's nations (some even start wars to benefit themselves).

5. All of this yet typically they never come to know Jesus or understand what happens when they die.

The folly of political leaders is clear to everyone (check the polls), but no one has solutions.

As a result, the poor can never break out of their position. In fact, their plight only gets worse. Those in public housing are at risk of becoming homeless, and their children bear an even higher risk. Even recent college graduates cannot find good work. Older managers who graduated from college decades ago are losing their jobs and are not able to find new good ones.

The most damaging effect, however, is the poor fearing loss of what little they have: crumbs doled out by government. Many feel they can never get married or get a job for fear of losing welfare/disability or any of the myriad of government benefits that keeps them enabled and entrapped.

The saddest of all? **The destruction of America's middle class**. Long the foundation and bastion of this powerful nation, the middle class is being systematically drowned by politics and business. (figures 16–21, pages 102–105) Unless we turn this around, it will kill our nation. Losing hope in being American is to lose our nation. And it's already all around us, happening with our eyes wide open.

IS GOD REALLY IN CONTROL?

The Bible certainly assures us that God is in control. The question is, does He want to control America's actions towards the poor? Let's revisit the foundational Scriptures for His sovereignty:

> *"I make known the end from the beginning, from ancient times, what is still to come. I say: My purpose will stand, and I will do all that I please. From the east I summon a bird of prey; from a far-off land, a man to fulfill my purpose. What I have said, that will I bring about; what I have planned, that will I do."* (Isaiah 46:10-11)

> *"And we know that God causes everything to work together for the good of those who love God and are called according to his purpose for them. For God knew his people in advance, and he chose them to become like his Son...."* (Romans 8:28-29)

God is certainly in control. Moreover, the poor are rich: *"Has not God chosen those who are poor in the eyes of the world to be **rich in faith** and to inherit the kingdom he promised those who love him?"* (Jas. 2:5). Therefore, God is orchestrating the humbling of America so that we'll become poor and rich in faith.

GOD IS WORKING GOOD FOR THE POOR

That America's poor groups are growing in number cannot be disputed. Whether this is God-orchestrated is uncertain. Those with strong faith, like Mother Teresa, don't need this to live their lives for the poor, the sick and the dying. She audibly heard His voice; she didn't need to know whether God was orchestrating poverty in India. But I am weak; I would not be able to even tie Mother Teresa's sandals.

Nonetheless, the focus of the church and for those who want to obey God: **Care for the poor.**

LIVING LIFE WITH YOUR POOR

This chapter was dedicated to answering the question, **What is God doing today?** He is orchestrating world events, especially in a busted America, to return all of our hearts to Him. He's allowing us to become poor in resources that we will be made rich in Him. That means we must care for the poor.

Jesus said: *"Feed my lambs...Take care of my sheep...Feed my sheep...Follow me"* (Jn. 21:16-19).

Jesus modeled the best way to minister to the poor: **Live life together.** Jesus lived life with His disciples until He died. Then He lived life with them after He rose again. Now He lives life with us through the Holy Spirit (Jn. 14:17).

Essentially, **live life with people**. How? By **living in community** (Acts 2:42-47): eating together, fellowshipping and learning about a living relationship with Jesus. This is His model for our churches. That model has died in the American church. So God is forcefully bringing it back. He wants to live with us by connecting us with our poor.

So, **who is our poor?**

And, once we know what God is doing: **What are we to do?**

CHAPTER 6

OUR MISSION:
WHAT DOES GOD WANT US TO DO?

"This is what the Lord says:
'When seventy years are completed for Babylon,
I will come to you and fulfill my gracious promise
to bring you back to this place.
For I know the plans I have for you,' declares the Lord,
'plans to prosper you and not to harm you,
plans to give you hope and a future.
Then you will call upon me and come and pray to me,
and I will listen to you.
You will seek me and find me when you seek me
with all your heart.
I will be found by you,' declares the Lord,
'and will bring you back from captivity.
I will gather you from all the nations and places where
I have banished you,' declares the Lord,
'and will bring you back to the place from which
I carried you into exile.'"
(Jeremiah 29:10-14)

GOD IS HUMBLING AMERICA; SO NOW WHAT?

God is humbling our nation so that He may humble us. The sooner we recognize that, the easier to trust Him; otherwise we'll pray counter to God's movement. God is allowing us to become poor so that we as a nation may work together again. Like America did in her early years. We're to help each other, starting with our families and immediate communities (neighborhoods, workplaces, churches, ministries). **God will accomplish His plan; we must humble ourselves and conform to His will**. He is testing us.

Our final question: *"What is God's mission for us?"* We'll answer this via the format of this book: Looking at the groups of poor and bringing relevant Scripture to determine how we (you) might live life with each one. Applications may differ individually, but the principles cross cultural and family lines.

As God humbles America, we'll **soon find ourselves a second-class nation**. We've become prideful and arrogant. We can see it in our leaders. In Congress. In our judicial system. In the IRS (I hope I don't get audited for this). In our rich business leaders. God is pulling (has pulled?) the plug on America's wealth, and all Americans will suffer. In God's Kingdom, suffering is when God does His best work.

If you are in one of the "poor groups" God is working good to humble you. How bad can that be; He's giving you a "makeover" to be more like Jesus. You can look at your loss of income or assets; your shrinking net worth and retirement; maybe you won't be able to retire when you had hoped or maybe you're forced to sell assets that were set aside for retirement to pay bills. You can focus on that, if you wish. Or you can recognize the truth: **To depend on God and become more like Jesus in humility (less pride) is priceless**. The suffering and pain will be worth it.

HOW CAN WE LIVE WITH JESUS?

God gives us a mission as part of His plan; His ultimate plan is for us to become like Jesus. We all have many things we can do that tie-in to the mission He gives us. The best way God sanctifies us is by living out our mission. It's how we see His Hand in our lives. And this in turn helps us to transform.

Jesus gave us our goal: *"Be perfect, therefore, as your heavenly Father is perfect"* (Mt. 5:48). He said this in the context of teaching us about agape love. The ultimate in perfection would be to love like Jesus, to have His humility and zero pride. None of us will ever be able to live perfect love this side of heaven. However, if Jesus walked with us daily through our challenges *in bodily form*, and interacted with us minute-by-minute over a 30-year period, we could make headway.

Though walking with Jesus in bodily form is not possible, God did provide a way: the **Holy Spirit** lives in us and Jesus is at the right hand of the Father interceding for us 24/7 (Rom. 8:34). Jesus wants to walk with us every step we take, so that our hearts will center on Him. This is the closest we'll get to perfection. As we do, we'll see His Hand *"caus[ing] all things"* to work together for good.

For me walking with Jesus consciously (about 5-10% of my time) helps me to know that He is always with me, no matter what. For example, when I lose stuff in cyberspace, I know God will use the loss to work out good for me. If Diana "bums me out" (rarely), I trust God will humble me or do something good in me. There is no situation where God is not working to improve some area of my life. And I am fertile ground for Jesus!

My goal is to walk with Jesus consciously more often (at least double, 10-20% of time).

CORRECTION KEEPS US ON TRACK

Christianity is a relationship with the Father through Jesus. To develop and grow that relationship, I have to stay on the journey He gave as my mission. Early on, I discovered I cannot live life with Jesus very effectively just sitting in my office or my prayer closet. Sure, spending quiet time with God is a blessing and He joins me there, in my thoughts. But I could never test if God was really interacting with me. In other words, I never seemed to know if they're just my thoughts or truly God's voice speaking to my heart. God shows up best and confirms His voice, timing, and direction when I walk it out.

> *"In his heart a man plans his course, but the Lord determines his steps."* (Proverbs 16:9)

God confirms we're on the right path when something good happens: an opportunity to connect with someone, seeing an old acquaintance, hearing a name from the past, and so forth.

But more often, for me at least, He often has course corrections while I'm walking: "A little more to the left; stop. Faster! Okay, a little more to the right; now look up at Me." He speaks in disciplinary steps. Allow me to share two memorable course corrections that helped me stay on mission:

1. NINJA CENTIPEDE BITE (2008)

Assignment: Help Hawaii Cedar Church (Korean Church)
Journey: On my way to becoming a pastor
Mission: Form a church and recognize God's call to pastor.

One night while sleeping, God sent something to bite me. I woke up in intense pain, whipped the blankets off, jumped out of bed, searching for what surely *had* to be a giant centipede. There was none. Still, my left foot was in excruciating pain. (I have low pain tolerance, Diana might have thought it was a mosquito bite.) There were two small bite marks but my foot was not swollen. Diana had to change the sheets and checked thoroughly for the centipede. It had disappeared; God had sent a "ninja centipede"!

(P.S. Don't ask Diana for her thoughts about that incident.)

At the time my electrical contracting business was my mission; but God revealed it was just my training ground and a means for His provisions to flow through. God wanted me to commit to my mission and go "all in," but I was resisting by delaying. He sent a messenger to wake me up!

It's like tithing, God is not so concerned with the tithe — time, talent and treasure — as He is with our heart to give the tithe. We show by giving cheerfully that we're fully committed, fully loving, fully trusting God. I needed a little prompting, so God sent a ninja centipede to give me a "love tap." That week I knew His desire clearly, and I could not have known had I not been on my journey. Also, I would not be a pastor today had I not obeyed.

2. STOCK MARKET HIT (LATE 2002) (figure 22, page 106)

Assignment: Build hedge fund as vehicle against stock market crash, which would hurt our company
Journey: On my way to provide funds for God's use
Mission: Build A-1 A-Lectrician into a strong, self-sustaining firm that could provide for God's programs.

Our A-1 hedge portfolio had a large boost due to the stock market crash that took place late 2000 through 2002. Our hedge portfolio made money if the market fell. However, if the stock market crashed, construction would be bad. So our hedge helped protect A-1 from a devastating fall and resultant slowdown. Our bankers hated the inherent risk in the portfolio.

The week of October 7, 2002 was monumental. The Standard and Poor's 500 index (SPX) had fallen 700 points from its peak. On Thursday, October 10, it kept falling and our portfolio peaked. However, within minutes, the SPX bottomed. During the next week, the S&P 500 turned around. Our hedge portfolio lost 25% of its peak value. It happened on my birthday; God was making a statement and giving me a birthday present: Humble pie. *Yummy!*

You see, the boost in our portfolio led to a boost in my pride. I started believing that I was brilliant, and shouldn't have to help with menial tasks around the house like wash dishes. (When you become proud you rationalize.) That next week, I was washing dishes and in awe of God.

COURSE CORRECTIONS FOR CHARACTER

In both cases, I had a special assignment on my journey towards God's global mission. God *"disciplines and punishes"* those He considers sons and daughters (Heb. 12:6). That way we won't get too far off track. God had something particular in mind and I would never have gotten that if I wasn't walking it out. He speaks through our circumstances. I knew each time what He wanted (the next step was clear), yet I was slow to take it. He's faithful to give an extra nudge.

It's like that old movie, "Indiana Jones and the Last Crusade." Adventure-hero Indy is on a journey, following a map. He picks his way delicately through an obstacle-laced walkway and survives, only to end up at the edge of a deep drop-off cliff. It's about 50-feet from the other side. There's no possible way Indy can jump it, even with his trusty whip.

Indy reexamines the map and concludes, "A leap of faith." His Dad replies, "You must believe, boy! You must believe!" Indy holds his breath and takes the only step he can, forward. He lifts his leg in an exaggerated motion (movies) and when his foot comes down, what should be sure death is suddenly an unseen bridge. Indy walks safely across.

God wants to guide our steps but He cannot do so if we are not walking forward.

WE HAVE BECOME SPOILED:
WE WAIT WHEN WE SHOULD WALK

Americans have become spoiled. We've been trained to wait for leaders, which only works if they are righteous, honorable men of integrity. So we should be concerned about electing righteous leaders. However, the greater impact might come not from waiting for the right leaders, but in leading your family and larger *'ohana* (community).

Mother Teresa said: "**Do not wait for leaders; do it alone, person to person.**"

There is a similar principle I follow: "**We intersect where we intersect**. We can't do everything together, but we can do some things together. I can't do everything you do, but I can do the things God called me to do with you."

This allows me to take on many assignments, walk my journey and not have to wait for a leader to pave the way. God is our leader and we must follow Him. When we are on our journey and follow Mother Teresa's principle, our connection with God will grow.

GOD WANTS UNITY — WALK TOWARDS IT

To impact Hawaii and our nation, **we must connect with movements directed by God**. That requires unity. If the people of Israel came out of Egypt and went in 500 different directions, there would not be a nation of Israel today. If we are to make a "God impact," we must be part of a movement that is not just one person. We must be **connected with a group of like-minded people on the same mission**.

However, don't sit and wait for the "right" group. Walk out your relationship with God, and as you do, the "streams" of God will connect you to others. God will make connections as you listen to Him.

One of the challenges I have in joining groups (church, business, or community) is that once they start, it's difficult for me to be involved in every aspect of their movement. It may be the same for you. Many are afraid to get a movement started, thinking, *If you help me, then I must help you.* There can be expectations: whether giving funds, time or effort. But consider: **God has His own plan**. Let God be God. You may not be involved in everything the leader wants, or you'll get burnt out. God guides us and does so through directing your involvement in His global mission.

For example: **People are at different stages in life**. If you are raising small children, they will take up most of your time and resources. If your kids are in high school, you may find yourself on your knees a lot. If your kids are young adults, you may be in a better position to get involved. Similarly, if you have elderly parents, God's journey is different for you. The key is this: **You need to hear from Him**.

Still, as Mother Teresa said, "Everyone can do something."

Jesus desires unity in any involvement (Jn. 17) so be involved as much as you can. For me, I've found what works is to be involved with many assignments but, as the work grows, I let God direct as to which ones to continue. I cannot let each assignment grow beyond time limits available in that season. So I'm continually asking God which one I must stop. That allows me to fully commit time and resources to the long-term journey that remains.

When we were raising kids and building our business in the 80s and 90s, that took first priority. As our kids got older (1990-2005), God drew us to Jesus and poured His love into us. He developed me in areas where He was calling me. My heart was in unity with my church leaders and I served the church.

Eventually (late 90s), First Assembly of God (thank you, Pastor Ko) allowed me to teach and develop my own curriculum. I remained connected with my church leaders, yet God called me outside the church to teach and eventually preach in many different ministries.

A large part of my Christian growth took place during this period as God expanded my reach by connecting me with different people. I look at all of the different people, groups, churches and parachurch ministries as under the umbrella of One Church. Honestly, it was difficult to be in unity with the many people God connected me to, yet that was always a desire.

For example, in the mid-90s, I started meeting with a small group of Christian leaders including pastors. There was one pastor whom I had met at an event and I invited him to join our group. He asked what the purpose was, I told him we got together for fellowship. He scoffed and said something to the effect that he wouldn't waste his time on "fellowshipping." It was tough finding common spiritual ground to stand in unity, but it's necessary because Jesus says so. I just kept walking.

LIVING LIFE WITH "OUR" POOR: SEEING THE GOOD

To see the good God is doing in our nation, in the poor, and in us, let's take a closer look at each group. We know God is humbling America by allowing our nation of fools (not you, you're reading this book) to destroy itself. As a result, we will end up poor and in different degrees of poverty. I've defined five groups of poor. (There are more but I chose these as business, family life, and ministry have connected me with these groups.) Let's start with a description of each one to give a springboard for our discussion:

1. THE HOMELESS POOR

These are people who live on the street. It also includes the soon-to-be homeless: those living in shelters and short-term rented rooms. This is not the homeless count made by state agencies.

2. THOSE IN POVERTY (BUT NOT HOMELESS)

This second group has rental units but is living below the poverty level, and survives on government subsidies: food stamps (S.N.A.P.), welfare, disability, Medicaid.

3. MIDDLE CLASS POOR (& HEADED TO POVERTY)

The third group is the middle class who are losing purchasing power, income, assets, and retirement. (Not all middle class fall into this group.) They will fall below the poverty level. The poverty level in Hawaii for a family of four is currently $23,850 - $27,430. They have little hope of breaking out of their condition and will struggle in their golden years. They'll end up working into their 70s. (U.S. Dept. of Health & Human Services 2014; http://aspe.hhs.gov/poverty/14poverty.cfm)

4. COLLEGE GRADUATES (THE "EDUCATED POOR")

The fourth group includes those who have graduated from college but do not have the jobs they were expecting. These include professionals (college-educated, white-collar workers) in their 50s and 60s who lost jobs in the last recession. They're having difficulty finding comparable jobs.

5. THE DYING POOR

The fifth group is really all people as we will all die. This includes anyone fearful of dying as well as the terminally ill who worry about living through the "dying experience." It includes those who have prolonged difficulty in their last years: pain, suffering, dementia, Alzheimer's, cancer or diabetes.

SILVOSO'S FOUR POVERTY TYPES

Evangelist Ed Silvoso sheds further light on the blight of the poor as he categorizes four types of poverty: *spiritual, relational, motivational* and *material*. Keep in mind that the five groups of poor focused upon in this book deal mainly with material poverty. Yet they may also lack in one or more of Silvoso's other types of poverty. Silvoso also recognizes that the rich can lack in spiritual and relational wealth:

"1. **Spiritual poverty** afflicts those who do not know that God is their father.

2. **Relational poverty** encompasses those whose focus is on themselves at the expense of the community they are a part of.

3. **Motivational poverty** is a state of hopelessness that engulfs those who have no adequate way or means (or the confidence) to tackle tomorrow's challenges.

4. **Material poverty** impacts those who lack the basic necessities to sustain themselves."

("Transformation," Ed Silvoso, Regal, Gospel Light, Ventura CA, p. 117)

HAWAII'S EPIC HOMELESS EPIDEMIC

Hawaii's main newspaper, the *Star-Advertiser*, now runs daily articles on our homeless population. The front-page coverage, political news, editorials, and plentiful pictures are constant reminders of the severity of the issue. Everyone has an opinion and a solution. The trouble is most try to sweep the homeless under a rug, where they cannot be seen or heard from again. "Solutions" include Housing First, tent cities, more toilet facilities, hotel rooms, and others. All are stopgap measures, bandaids for heartbreak.

My humble opinion? Allow me to draw a comparison to medical treatment. If you can't move your bowels, you don't just start drilling.

If blood comes out in your urine (let's get real), you don't simply plug it up. You must find the source of the problem.

What is the source of the homeless problem?

Fools!

Fools are running our government. (God's definition, not name-calling.)

The Bible tells us to *"submit to the governing authorities"* and I'm not suggesting otherwise. God says He establishes all authority structures and we are to obey the laws of the land, except where they conflict with God's laws.

Another source of the homeless problem is that we (who elected the fools) have destroyed hope and motivation in the souls of people by "enabling" them through government subsidies.

GONE: THE AMERICAN DREAM & OUR MIDDLE CLASS

When I was growing up, there were very few homeless. I thought they were "drunks and bums" who just laid around on dirty streets and hid in parks. I was young, very judgmental, and a fool then.

At about this time the government started greatly increasing programs: public housing, welfare, medical care and disability. Pretty soon those "in need" no longer needed: They had become entirely dependent on government. The government meant well, but **good intentions of a fool can destroy**.

Something died during this era: the hard-working American. America was built on the backs of people who came from other countries that lacked opportunity. They came for the American dream, which was fully obtainable. That is no longer true.

AN UP-CLOSE-&-PERSONAL STUDY
OF THE HOMELESS

Our church has a good cross section of the poor. During any one-month period, we may have 60% homeless or living in shelters. Some of these have income, some do not. Most have food stamps.

Now, I have not done a scientific study of our people, nor do I intend to. My analysis is in knowing my sheep (congregation). Many of the homeless today grew up in public housing. Some grew up in normal or good homes and ended up running with the wrong crowd; some spent time in prison. Many did drugs or alcohol. Some still do, occasionally (so they claim). It's hard to know for sure as they tend to disappear for a time. Our goal is to provide a place that draws them to Jesus, no matter their condition.

My conclusion is **many who have grown up in public housing end up in public housing**. (Not all.) Many of their children end up homeless. (Not all.) Many live transient lives. They stay with someone they love, someone they know, or someone they hate, but have no choice. These are "**hidden homeless**." Some live in a living room with friends or, if they can afford to, rent a room. These rentals range from $200 (slum) to $500 (Kalihi). They can go from a room to homeless overnight, then possibly end up in another room somewhere else the next day. They stay wherever they can with whoever will take them in. It's a hard life. I don't judge them.

Women who live this way have it rough. Their lifestyle is often fast: sex, drugs and alcohol are common. Rape and incest is normal for many (not all). When you grow up this way, you see life differently. Their culture is different. I do not judge. I know Jesus is the Answer, so I preach Jesus and the Bible, but I cannot change them. Only God can.

Many of these women need the protection of a man for physical safety, emotional support and financial security. Many have had multiple men and multiple kids. These kids have many "uncles." The next man in Mom's life is an "uncle." Women who have kids are entitled to welfare and food stamps. The more kids, the more funds. All love their kids but cannot marry the father; not because they don't know which one they love, but because they'll lose funding. We've "enabled" them. Those who have enough kids get into public housing or an apartment unit through Section 8. They can make it if they smoke their dollar bills. They're trapped in the cycle, enslaved in the system.

Unattached men fall into two groups: Those who have disability checks and those who do not. Those with disability checks collect about $700 per month, plus food stamps and medical coverage. Some are homeless, some are not. They make a choice: They can hook up with a woman. However, many women cannot marry them for fear of losing benefits. And the benefits are more stable than the men.

Many of these men go to a professional who signs off that they are disabled, in accordance with laws for disability. These professionals earn a good living by qualifying their "patients" for seasonal checkups. They just have to prove they're disabled. And the government of "fools" passes laws to help them. They ask each other, "Tell me what I have to do! Tell me what I have to say." They get their checks; the professionals, too.

Some "disabled" look normal, but who's to say what is normal. Many could work, but why when someone pays you to do nothing. I certainly am not qualified (by law) to determine who can work. I don't have the license. Who gives out the license? Who made the laws? Fools. America is busted.

KNOWLEDGE VS. WISDOM

Knowledge tells us that America is busted. Knowledge knows something is wrong with the system. Knowledge knows the homeless are suffering. Knowledge knows that many around the homeless are also suffering. Yet knowledge doesn't tell us what to do.

Wisdom tells us we need to do something. My sense tells me that **God is the Answer, and has the answer. This is the first step in wisdom, trusting God for His plan.** Since God is causing America's demise, fixing is not possible; things will get worse. Our main focus becomes helping the poor.

So I plow forward at Cedar AOG to bring Jesus to the people stuck in this system.

CAN LOVE BE THE ULTIMATE TEST?

Homeless are people too; and God loves them. I used to think the homeless deserved what they got for their irresponsibility. But the Bible doesn't give conditions that excuse us from helping the poor. It doesn't give us a way out. Why should we help people who don't help themselves? Jesus died for them.

Jesus warned, *"Because of the increase of wickedness, the love of most will grow cold, but he who stands firm to the end will be saved"* (Mt. 24:12-13). Don't let your unconditional agape cool your passion for Christ or for those whom He has compassion.

Wisdom is not attaching conditions to the homeless for their choices. I am not saying Christians should take them into their homes (although Jesus would, except that Jesus was also homeless. But we're not Jesus. Aha, so we have a way out; thank God for grace!) But it is about doing something.

IS GOD "CONNECTING THE DOTS"?

The homeless maintain strong relationships with each other. They'll give their last $20 to help someone in an emergency. This is similar to the Old Testament where it was customary to show hospitality and take in traveling strangers, even in your tent or home. The idea is to help someone in need and then one day someone will help you when you are traveling. Homeless show similar "hospitality" in helping each other.

On the other hand, very few of us with homes, cars, jobs, and savings would give all we have to help someone in an emergency. Granted, it's a different scale, but the principle remains: **The homeless have strong relationships with others**. The poor can lose all they have and still have friends.

The wealthy have many "friends," but rarely any unconditional relationships. In fact, the wealthy who lose all they have lose all their friends. Most are bonded only through wealth. If the wealth is gone, the bonds are broken. (Not for all.)

Could God be trying to connect the two groups?

Ed Silvoso makes a case that both groups have what the other group needs: "Generally speaking, the poor score higher on the spiritual and relational dimensions, because faith in God is often the only source of hope available to survive the hopelessness that engulfs them, and relationships are a vital part of that survival mechanism. On the other hand, people of wealth fare better on the material and motivational aspects. They have resources and the attitude and the know-how to leverage them so as not to approach the future with desperation, but they tend to score lower on relationships, and their faith in God is usually more 'professional' than personal.

"By coming together, both groups were able to minister to each other in their respective areas of need. The rich found fellowship and were inspired by the resilient faith of the poor, while the poor benefited from material things made available by the rich and their sense of hope for the future." ("Transformation," Ed Silvoso, p. 124)

God knows this and is creating of all of these poor groups so Americans may help one another.

LITERALLY JESUS, REALLY?

"For I was hungry and you gave me something to eat, I was thirsty and you gave me something to drink, I was a stranger and you invited me in, I needed clothes and you clothed me, I was sick and you looked after me, I was in prison and you came to visit me. Then the righteous will answer him, 'Lord, when did we see you hungry and feed you, or thirsty and give you something to drink? When did we see you a stranger and invite you in, or needing clothes and clothe you? When did we see you sick or in prison and go to visit you?' The King will reply, 'I tell you the truth, whatever you did for one of the least of these brothers of mine, you did for me.'"
(Matthew 25:35-40)

Jesus said, *"You gave me...invited me...clothed me...looked after me... came to visit me...."* Could Jesus *literally* mean *"me"*? God is Spirit. And the Holy Spirit lives in strangers who are hungry, thirsty, naked, and sick. **Could Jesus Himself be receiving our kindness as we help *"the least of these"*?**

COMPASSION: ULTIMATE PATH OF LOVE

Compassion may be the most under-lived trait in the Christian Church today. (And I put myself at the top of the list of those short on compassion. God wired me tough. As a businessman I often had to make tough calls. Had God given me an overdose of compassion, our company might have failed long ago.)

Jesus loves people and has compassion for us. Apostles Matthew, Mark, and Luke all wrote of many instances in Jesus' life where compassion was the change agent of miracles:

"When he saw the crowds, he had compassion on them, because they were harassed and helpless, like sheep without a shepherd."
(Matthew 9:36)

"When Jesus landed and saw a large crowd, he had compassion on them and healed their sick." (Matthew 14:14)

"Jesus called his disciples to him and said, 'I have compassion for these people; they have already been with me three days and have nothing to eat. I do not want to send them away hungry, or they may collapse on the way.'" (Matthew 15:32)

"Jesus had compassion on them and touched their eyes. Immediately they received their sight and followed him." (Matthew 20:34)

"Filled with compassion, Jesus reached out his hand and touched the man. 'I am willing,' he said. 'Be clean!' Immediately the leprosy left him and he was cured." (Mark 1:41-42)

"When Jesus landed and saw a large crowd, he had compassion on them, because they were like sheep without a shepherd. So he began teaching them many things." (Mark 6:34)

"Not long after that, the younger son got together all he had, set off for a distant country and there squandered his wealth in wild living. After he had spent everything, there was a severe famine in that whole country, and he began to be in need. So he went and hired himself out to a citizen of that country, who sent him to his fields to feed pigs. He longed to fill his stomach with the pods that the pigs were eating, but no one gave him anything.
"When he came to his senses, he said, 'How many of my father's hired men have food to spare, and here I am starving to death! I will set out and go back to my father and say to him: Father, I have sinned against heaven and against you. I am no longer worthy to be called your son; make me like one of your hired men.' So he got up and went to his father. But while he was still a long way off, his father saw him and was filled with compassion for him; he ran to his son, threw his arms around him and kissed him." (Luke 15:13-20)

The definition of **compassion** from the Merriam-Webster dictionary: "sympathetic consciousness of others' distress together with a desire to alleviate it."

What "distresses" did those people have? Jesus described them as: *"harassed and helpless," "sick," "hungry…or may collapse," "blind,"* a man with leprosy, and *"like sheep without a shepherd."* With the prodigal son, Jesus recognized that he had become destitute in every way.

What did Jesus feel when He had compassion for these people? (Don't say, "Compassion," that's circular talk.) What *emotion* did He feel, sadness? (I'm bummed that I do *not* feel.)

Is agape love different from compassion? Why is compassion not mentioned in the "love chapter" (1 Cor. 13)? Is it not love? I've never thought much about compassion. I read about it in the Bible but as a "buffet Christian," I skip it and not worry whether I'm living it or not. However, now that I am thinking about it, I have to conclude: **Compassion requires love, but is different from love**.

Love is an action that we live: We can be patient, gentle and kind, not envious, not easily angered, not rejoicing in evil, trusting, hoping and persevering… but none of these seem to be compassion. **Compassion requires me to see others' distress and desire to help them**. Compassion requires love, but is distinct from love. **Love affects how we live. Compassion affects others**. Perhaps their combination completes God's Love for us.

As I analyze my life, I've either shied away from people requiring compassion, or I've rationalized against helping. I moved away from those who had needs and attempted to cling to me. When I interacted with them, sure I acted with love, but that's a natural reaction. The *compassion* Jesus had caused Him to actively move towards people with needs.

Part of my rationalization is that I was focused on agape love. Compassion never seemed to fit nicely into love so I never bothered with it. So when I came to Paul writing, *"Praise be to the God and Father of our Lord Jesus Christ, the Father of compassion..."* (2 Cor. 1:3), I **still** focused elsewhere: On God the Father and Lord Jesus. But if God is the *"Father of compassion,"* is it something He wants to impart?

COMPASSION APPLIED

If we're like Jesus, what *feeling* do we have when we see the homeless on the streets?

Do we wonder, "Where do they take a dump? How do they feel when they dump on the sidewalk? Do they wipe?" (Side note: I was teaching a study at Salvation Army and giving out my book, "God's Hand in the Life of an Electrician" to John. I joked, "Eh, guys, don't use this to wipe!" John didn't laugh. It's only funny if you don't have to do that.)

Are we compassionate or just upset that they're taking dumps in public areas? Aren't we supposed to help alleviate their situation? I know I cannot help all of them (6,000 plus Hawaii homeless) but do I even care? Compassion cares. What does that look like?

When we hear of public housing kids who cause trouble, do drugs, and steal, are we upset at them and disgusted at their parents? Or do we have compassion? What would that look like?

If we say we love God, Jesus, and others, does that love cause us to do something? I realize we cannot help all but that's not the issue. **Do we have compassion? Do we really love as Jesus loved?**

Can we have compassion for the homeless without solving their problem?

Too many questions! (My head hurts; but not my heart. I'm wretched.)

FIXING THE NATION OR FIXING OUR ATTITUDES?

As Christians, we recognize the homeless problem cannot be fixed without God. Fools in government need to do something so they pass laws to push the homeless out of desirable areas. As fools do, they convince themselves they can kick the can down the road. They only do enough to stop people from shouting, "Get them off my streets! Get them away from my entry! Get them away from my kids! Get them away!" However, there is no getting away from the underlying problem. People are in dire need.

There's a story about an old man who went fishing with the game warden. They were friends and the warden wondered how his friend always caught more fish than anyone. They reached their fishing spot and the old man pulled out a stick of dynamite and threw it overboard. **KABOOOM!** Dozens of fish floated up. The warden was shocked and told his friend, "You can't do that!" The old man lit another stick of dynamite, handed it to the warden, and asked, "You gonna fish or yap all day?"

Does God want us to yap all day or act His way?

LIVE LIFE WITH YOUR POOR

Let's look at what compassion might look like with the different groups of poor:

1. HOMELESS — LIVE LIFE WITH THEM

If you have a friend or relative who is struggling with homelessness, drugs or alcohol, pray and ask God what He wants of you. If He says to pray, then pray. If He says to give to a program that helps people with these struggles (like Salvation Army or Teen Challenge) then give. It doesn't have to be much. He just wants us to love and have His compassion.

If you are able, and He wants you to take in one of your friends or relatives stuck in drugs, then obey Him. First ask the hard questions: Who? When? How? Seek counsel with your pastor or other Christians. Or you can offer him an incentive: If he quits, goes into a drug rehab program, and graduates, then he can move in with you for 3 months (or 6 months) so he can get a job. You might give him an incentive like $1,000 at the end of whatever milestone God tells you. $1,000 for a new soul to have a chance at a new life? You might feel God's pleasure raining down on you even if you get scammed. There is no failure if you trust God through your ordeal.

If someone in your family is caught up in drugs and alcohol, theft and/or lying; maybe you can have love and compassion for him. So that when he comes around, what would God want from you? It's hard as you don't want to enable him. But yelling, swearing, and telling him, "I told you so" is no longer an option. What would compassion look like?

2. PUBLIC HOUSING – LIVE LIFE WITH THEM

If you know (or are connected to) someone in public housing and struggling to make ends meet, you might consider adopting them. Or visit them! Yes, in their apartments or rooms, if that's where they live. They're in all of our churches. Apply the same outreach as the guy stuck in drugs. People need to know someone cares and will walk with them; someone who loves them and can bring agape into their lives. Not many have experienced the agape love of Jesus. Maybe that's why people struggle. Somehow, a government worker, no matter how sincere, is not the same. They are paid to do the job. Show true love.

3. MIDDLE CLASS HEADED FOR POVERTY – LIVE LIFE WITH THEM

If you know someone in the middle class struggling with two jobs and out-of-control kids, ask God what you might do. They are in our churches and workplaces. You may not be able to tell because they're always smiling in church. But ask yourself: *How does a single mother with a decent job handle two kids when they get sick and her car breaks down? Who helps her?*

Ask God, *Who?* He'll show you. They're the ones that complain and always need help. They want to borrow money, drink or smoke dope, and you run when they come. Jesus wouldn't run.

How does Jesus see them? They need help. If you have time, resources, talent, maybe God has entrusted them to your care but you've been too busy judging and criticizing them. I know I do that. Jesus wouldn't. He died for them. I fall short. Maybe you do too. Who knows but you are the one person that might help them make a radical transformation. It might take one year. It might take five. The more time it takes, the more God needs you. The more you will see His Hand actively showing up.

4. COLLEGE GRADUATES – LIVE LIFE WITH THEM

There are many college graduates that will not have their job expectations fulfilled. Over the next 10 years, I estimate only 60-80% will be working in a job they like. That leaves 20-40% out in the cold. That may mean 5-10 million working as waiters, hotel clerks, fast food operators, taxi drivers, or other entry level positions. These low-paying jobs are well below what college graduates made 20 years ago.

They may have self-esteem issues and hopelessness which combined can destroy motivation. They may possibly end up homeless in 10 or 20 years. What might God be doing? How can He use you to work good in their lives? Refresh your spirit in the hundredfold blessing:

> *"'I tell you the truth,' Jesus replied, 'no one who has left home or brothers or sisters or mother or father or children or fields for me and the gospel will fail to receive a hundred times as much in this present age (homes, brothers, sisters, mothers, children and fields — and*

with them, persecutions) and in the age to come, eternal life. But many who are first will be last, and the last first.'" (Mark 10:29-31)

God is bringing families together. College kids are moving back home, as they have no other choice. In Hawaii, the 'ohana culture makes this easier than the mainland. There families are separated by state lines, many thousands of miles apart.

THE "BOOMERANG GENERATION"?

An interesting article entitled, "Here's Exactly How Many College Graduates Live Back at Home," says: "The unemployed college graduate moving back in with his parents has been a stock figure of the past few years, helping to cement the Millennials' reputation as the **'Boomerang Generation.'** But how many young grads are returning to live with their mom and dad (or their aunt or uncle)? The number to remember is 45%. What share of recent college graduates were living with family in 2011? It's 45%. How much higher was that figure than in 2001? Also 45%. That's the conclusion from Census data crunched for The Atlantic by Pew economist Richard Fry, the author of a recent report on young adults and debt. It's bad -- about on par with the unfortunate results Pew found via a poll of young adults in 2012." (The Atlantic, Jordan Weissmann, Feb 26 2013)

And another article in the "U.S. News & Word Report," confirms: "The number of college graduates working minimum wage jobs is nearly 71% higher than it was a decade ago, according to the Bureau of Labor Statistics' latest figures. As of 2012, 284,000 college graduates were working at or below the minimum wage, up from 167,000 in 2002 and more than two times the pre-recession low of 127,000 in 2006. The cohort includes an estimated 30,000 people with masters' degrees, a figure that is more than twice as high as it was in 2002 and three times as high as in 2006." (U.S. News & World Report, by Danielle Kurtzleben, Dec. 5, 2013)

And "The Atlantic" reports: "About 1.5 million, or 53.6%, of bachelor's degree-holders under the age of 25 last year were jobless or underemployed, the highest share in at least 11 years. In 2000, the share was at a low of 41%, before the dot-com bust erased job gains for college graduates in the telecommunications and IT fields. Out of the 1.5 million who languished in the job market, about half were underemployed, an increase from the previous year." ("The Atlantic," Jordan Weissmann, April 23, 2012)

Finally, an earlier excerpt from Paul Craig Robert's book, "The Failure of Laissez Faire Capitalism," projected that between the years 2007-2014, 8 million college graduates would be chasing after approximately 1.4 million jobs requiring a college degree. He also presents the case that "offshoring" of American production capacity is "destroying entire industries, occupations and communities in the United States. The devastation of U.S. manufacturing employment was waved away and dismissed with promises that a 'new economy' based on high tech knowledge jobs would take its place...."

SPIRITUAL FALLOUT

These many millions of unemployed or, more accurately, "*underemployed*" graduates will be injured soul-wise. They may become "poor in spirit": emotionally-damaged, low motivation, and materially poor. Many have been brainwashed by their "advanced education" that there is no God. Or at best they're agnostics who do not believe they may have a personal relationship with God.

But God has not forgotten them; He still loves them and draws them to His Son. And He wants to use you. So if you are a parent, be prepared. Think about asking God: **What does agape and compassion look like to them?** (from their point-of-view, really from God's point-of-view). Don't be ragging and nagging, moaning on and on about how much you spent on their education. Do not ask, *"What's wrong with you?"*

God is working for good for them and He wants to involve you. What an honor! He chose you to serve your children. What a privilege that you can serve Jesus; give Him water, food, clothes, visit them in their prisons (their rooms), and help His/their healing.

RECENT JOB LOSSES

Another group of college graduates that will "hurt big time" have had good jobs most of their lives but lost them in the last five years and have yet to find decent jobs. They did not save enough to retire and have not yet paid off their homes. They sacrificed for their children's college education. They may have run up their credit cards and refinanced their homes. They cannot ask their kids for help. Their medical coverage under ObamaCare is more expensive than before so they have to choose which bills to pay and which coverages to take. They have big trouble ahead.

Can you come alongside one of these and be a light to them?

COLLEGE GRADS WILL NEED MUCH SUPPORT

"Didn't I tell you, don't raise my hope?" This was what the Shunammite woman said to Elisha when her son died (2 Kings 4:28). It's exactly what an entire generation of our top-educated collegiates are asking.

Malcolm Gladwell wrote an interesting book, "David and Goliath." In it he presents the concept of 'relative deprivation': "a term coined by sociologist Samuel Stouffer during the Second World War. Stouffer was commissioned by the U.S. Army to examine the attitudes and morale of American soldiers, and he ended up studying half a million men and women, looking at everything from how soldiers viewed their commanding officers to how black soldiers felt they were being treated....

"He quizzed both soldiers serving in the Military Police and those serving in the Air Corps (the forerunner of the Air Force) about how good a job they thought their service did in recognizing and promoting people of ability. The answer was clear. Military Policemen (MP) had a far more positive view of their organization than did enlisted men in the Air Corps.

"On the face of it, that made no sense. The MP had one of the worst rates of promotion in all of the armed forces. The Air Corps had one of the best. The chance of an enlisted man rising to officer status in the Air Corps was twice that of a soldier in the MP. So why on earth would the MP be more satisfied? The answer is that MP compared themselves only to other MP. And if you got a promotion in the MP, that was such a rare event that you were very happy. And if you didn't get promoted, you were in the same boat as most of your peers—so you weren't that unhappy.

"The Air Corps...chance of getting promoted to officer was greater than 50%.... If (the Air Corpsman) failed to earn a rating while the majority had succeeded, he had more reason to feel a sense of personal frustration....

"Stouffer's point is that we form our impressions not globally, by placing ourselves in the broadest possible context, but locally—by comparing ourselves to people 'in the same boat as ourselves.' Our sense of how deprived we are is relative...."

Gladwell concludes that countries with a higher suicide rate are the countries that people declare themselves to be happy (Switzerland, Denmark, Canada). Countries whose citizens describe themselves as not very happy (Greece, Italy, Portugal, Spain) have a lower suicide rate. Gladwell says, "If you are depressed in a place where most people are pretty unhappy, you compare yourself to those around you and you don't feel all that bad. But can you imagine how difficult it must be to be depressed in a country where everyone else has a big smile on their face?" ("David and Goliath," Malcolm Gladwell, p. 77-78, Little, Brown & Co., NY)

Our college graduate group of "poor" will have huge challenges, huge barriers to overcome, and huge needs — spiritual, motivational, relational, and material. They will soon be emotionally worse off than those who've been in poverty all of their lives. Their hopes have crashed and burned.

They are a huge mission field for Christians and for their own families.

5. THE DYING POOR – LIVE LIFE WITH THEM

"There is a time for everything, and a season for every activity under heaven: a time to be born and a time to die." (Ecclesiastes 3:1-2)

Everyone dies. God took my Dad 35 years ago, Diana's Mom 20 years ago, and her Dad about 13 years ago. My Mom is in the process of being "promoted to glory" (a Salvation Army term). What might love and compassion look like for her? How might I live better for my Mom each day? If Jesus were to grade my love and compassion, what grade would He give me?

THE CYCLE OF LIFE

I have a crazy theory on the cycle of life. (If you're still reading this, you know I'm not crazy, just different. I hope my wife agrees.) We begin as a babies and grow into productive adults. We raise a family, work, build businesses and homes then slow down for our "golden years," retirement. We become slower, even slower, until we become babies again. Three years old, 1 year old, 6 months old, 3 months old, 1 month, 2 weeks, then one day, God takes us. Knowing this cycle helps me deal with my Mom's situation.

The Bible warns us that *"man is destined to die"* (Heb. 9:27). God knows exactly when, where, and how He will take us. God is causing our bodies to work for good, taking us to meet His Son, Jesus Christ, face to face. Paul looked at it this way:

> *"To live is Christ and to die is gain. If I am to go on living in the body, this will mean fruitful labor for me. Yet what shall I choose? I do not know! I am torn between the two: I desire to depart and be with Christ, which is better by far; but it is more necessary for you that I remain in the body. Convinced of this, I know that I will remain, and I will continue with all of you for your progress and joy in the faith, so that through my being with you again your joy in Christ Jesus will overflow on account of me."* (Philippians 1:21-26)

Dietrich Bonhoeffer, on death, wrote: "We surprise ourselves by the calmness with which we hear of the death of one of our contemporaries… We still love life, but I do not think that death can take us by surprise now. After what we have been through during the war, we hardly dare admit that we should like death to come to us, not accidentally and suddenly through some trivial cause, but in the fullness of life and with everything at stake. **It is we ourselves, and not outward circumstances, who make death what it can be, a death freely and voluntarily accepted.**" ("Bonhoeffer: Pastor, Martyr, Prophet, Spy," p. 477, Eric Metaxas, 2010, Thomas Nelson)

Very few can embrace death the way Apostle Paul and Dietrich Bonhoeffer did. Yet we can be prepared to "freely and voluntarily accept it." Bonhoeffer emphasized, "It is we ourselves, and not [anything else]" that make death what it is.

As I write this, my Mom is now between 3 years old and 1 year old (in my theorized life cycle). She has good days and bad days. I cry as I realize she will not read this book, but I rejoice in my tears because she will honor the promise she made to Dad when God took him 35 years ago: "Daddy, go with God. Go with God when you're ready. Go to heaven, build our new home and wait for us. We'll all come when it's our time. Wait for us, okay, Daddy?"

The good thing with God's life cycle is that He allows illness (cancer, heart disease, etc.) to serve notice to our family and community that He's preparing to take us. This involves pain, suffering, turmoil, but it also gives the family and community time to say goodbye. There are hardships, many hardships, but they only last a year, maybe two, maybe five. What is that compared to eternity? Is Jesus enough to get us through? If not, you need more Jesus time. Me too.

Ending on a bright note: When your time comes, none of the issues in this book will concern you. You will be "In God's Hands."

A SWEET SWAN SONG

As I reflect on the "final chapter" of life in this final chapter of the book, I remember a particular family birthday dinner for Diana. We always honor the birthday baby with a special sharing time. I shared about how I had been an alcoholic in the 70s and 80s (quit '87) and Diana had stood by my side. Our family would have been very different had Diana left me; but she didn't even criticize or complain. She was a solid force of love throughout our ordeal.

The next day, our firstborn son, Daven, returned with a CD of a song he had written that night, complete with music. It followed what I had shared:

"LOVE OF MY LIFE"

Through the changes in my heart, changes in my mind
You were devoted, time after time
Through ten whole years, of my drinking times
You didn't walk out on me, to chase another life

CHORUS:

And I say thank you, love of my life
Forever grateful to the Lord, that you're still by my side
Ain't no joke, no exaggeration, no small thing in my mind
Without you I wouldn't be here today, your love in my life
In my life

I tried to chase so many dreams, your dreams became mine
Never counting the little things, you do each day of life
The sacrifices that you've made, I don't understand at all
Where we are on this day, you're more than a part of it all

CHORUS

You've given me two boys, a girl
Greatest gift of all
A family together in this world
Your heart holding it all

CHORUS

(by Daven Yamada)

Diana and I were so touched at the goodness of God in this, His work. Essentially we have a song that I may very well sing at Diana's funeral. (I am not morbid. My prayer is that God take Diana first so that I can take care of her in her last days. Not because I owe her, but because I love God and trust He'll give me strength and wisdom to walk through this.) This song is God's gift to us.

Diana's unconditional love was a vessel through which I learned God's love. Even when I was a wretch, she loved me and God loved me. And it is this love that I attempt to work out in myself and work out for others who are "poor;" as I too was once destitute.

Do I have all the answers? No, I am learning. But I do have the Answer, Jesus!

187

And we're walking forward.

My prayer is that God uses this sharing to inspire you in His great action plan of Love.

The greatest work for us is in us: *Can we have the love and compassion of Jesus?*

Will Christians be ready for this great move of God?

OTHER BOOKS BY JIMMY YAMADA

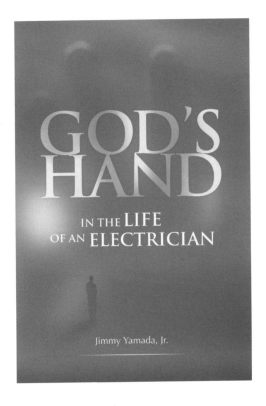

GOD'S HAND IN THE LIFE OF AN ELECTRICIAN (2008)

A great gift is to see God's hand on your life. In this life memoir, Jimmy Yamada, Jr. – a prominent Hawai'i businessman and ministry leader – looks back at the jagged shards of his past to see a clear pattern of God's design. And like sun streaming through a stained-glass cathedral, God truly makes all things good in His time. If God can do this for Jimmy Yamada, Jr., He can surely do it for you!

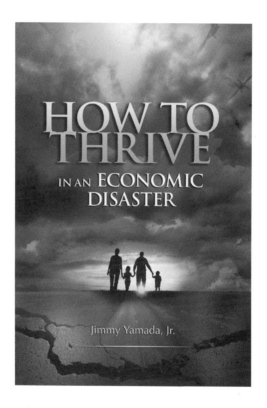

HOW TO THRIVE IN AN ECONOMIC DISASTER (2015)

Discover...

- Ways to prepare for a financial disaster
- Principles to help maneuver through your own calamities
- How God uses pain and suffering to develop strength and character
- Inspiring examples to apply lessons to your daily life

WHITE
MOUNTAIN
CASTLE
PUBLISHING, LLC

www.whitemountaincastle.com